GREAT EXPECTATIONS
by Charles Dickens
adapted by Tanika Gupta

First performed at Watford Palace Theatre
from 17 February - 12 March 2011

Cast (in alphabetical order)

Abel Magwitch	Jude Akuwudike
Compeyson	Rob Compton
Herbert Pocket	Giles Cooper
Jaggers	Russell Dixon
Miss Havisham	Lynn Farleigh
Mrs Gargery/Molly	Pooja Ghai
Pumblechook/Speaker	Shiv Grewal
Estella	Simone James
Joe Gargery	Tony Jayawardena
Pip	Tariq Jordan
Wemick	Darren Kuppan
Biddy	Kiran Landa

Director	Nikolai Foster
Designer	Colin Richmond
Lighting Designer	Lee Curran
Composer	Nicki Wells
Musical Advisor	Nitin Sawhney
Sound Designer	Sebastian Frost
Choreographer/Movement	Zoobin Surty
Movement	Cressida Carré
Associate Director	Nicola Samer
Fight Director	Kate Waters
Casting Director	Kay Magson CDG
Voice Coach	Tim Charrington
Deputy Stage Manager	Emma Hansford
Assistant Stage Manager	Ian Grigson
Prop Makers	Samantha Ford
	Sarah-Jane Davis
Wardrobe Assistants	Marny Clulow
	Hannah Marshall
Dressers	Marny Clulow
	Ruby Makin
Havisham dressmaker	Robbie Gordon
Wigs	Shepperton Wig Company

Great Expectations

Tanika Gupta introduces her adaptation

Of all the Dickens novels I read as a youth, Great Expectations was always a favourite. From the opening pages of Pip's terrifying encounter with Abel Magwitch in the graveyard, the novel's compelling story and Pip's momentous life journey had me gripped. This was a story I could absolutely relate to because of the aspiration of the main character, Pip, to rise above his class and status and to be educated. It was what my 24-year-old father aspired to when he left Calcutta in 1961 and sailed from Bombay to England, with the obligatory £1 note in his pocket.

In this stage adaptation of the novel, I relocated the action of the play to India of 1861 which meant that I could use Dickens' language without having to worry about modernising it. But I didn't want to do a straight forward 'Asian' adaptation. So, Magwitch is now a black convict from Cape Colony. He is not a slave (as slavery was abolished by the British by 1861), but an African sailor with a criminal background. His story, as in the original, is one borne of poverty and degradation, but in this adaptation, his anger at the white man's treatment of the black man lends an added fury. He is determined to make Pip into 'an English gentleman' who will be able to hold his head high. Miss Havisham, the lawyer Jaggers and Herbert Pocket all represent the different English facets of the Raj, whilst Joe Gargery (now a cobbler), Pip and Biddy are Indian villagers.

During the early part of the British Raj, Calcutta was the capital city and Pip journeys there to begin his education as an English gentleman. I was fascinated by the way the Colonial British authorities in India educated Indians of 'good families' in a very English way, encouraging them to embrace English values and morals. It wasn't an accident that Jawaharlal Nehru (The First Prime Minister of India) and Mohammed Ali Jinnah (The first Governor General of Pakistan) qualified as barristers in London and then went back to India to fight for their country's independence.

Ultimately, Pip's dissatisfaction at the way he is treated by the English leads him to question their wisdom and awakens his Indian pride.

Whilst Pip loses a lot at the end of the play (Estella, Magwitch and his inheritance), he gains a life-long friend in the quintessentially English Herbert Pocket. It is this friendship across the races which gives us hope and which propels us forward into the present day.

Tanika Gupta
February 2011

Acknowledgement: The author would like to thank Indhu Rubasingham for her help in realising this adaptation in the early stages of its development.

Great Expectations

PR
6057
U6
G74
201

ACT I

Scene 1
A Crematorium, Outside
A Village Near Calcutta. 1861.

Scene 2
A Village Near Calcutta

Scene 3
The Crematorium

Scene 4
The Crematorium. Kali Puja.

Scene 5
In The Village

Scene 6
The Journey To Miss Havisham's House

Scene 7
Outside The Gargery Hut

Scene 8
Miss Havisham's House

Scene 9
Miss Havisham's Garden

Scene 10
A Riverbank Near The Village

Scene 11
Miss Havisham's House

Scene 12
By The River

Scene 13
In The Village

Scene 14
Outside The Gargery Hut,
Five Years Later - 1866.

Scene 15
In The Village

Scene 16
Miss Havisham's House

INTERVAL

ACT II

Scene 1
The Streets Of Calcutta And Later,
Jaggers' Office

Scene 2
Herbert Pocket's Lodgings – Calcutta

Scene 3
A Café In Calcutta

Scene 4
Pocket's Lodgings

Scene 5
Pocket's Lodgings

Scene 6
Pocket's Lodgings

Scene 7
Miss Havisham's House

Scene 8
A Street In Calcutta

Scene 9
A Hideout In Calcutta

Scene 10
Miss Havisham's House

Scene 11
Jaggers' Office

Scene 12
The Streets Of Calcutta. Kali Puja.

Scene 13
A Prison Cell In Calcutta

Scene 14
The Village, Near Calcutta

Scene 15
The Streets Of Calcutta.
10 Years Later. 1876.

Cast Biographies

Jude Akuwudike Abel Magwitch
Jude trained at RADA. His most recent work in the theatre includes
Othello for Glasgow Citizens Theatre; Iya-Ile for Tiata Fahodzi/Soho
Theatre; Walking Waterfall at Tiata Delights '08, Almeida Theatre;
The Resistible Rise of Arturo Ui at the Lyric Hammersmith, Anthony
Nielson's God in Ruins at the Soho Theatre; Macbeth and Macbett
(RSC); The Overwhelming, Edmond and Henry V (National Theatre)
and Pericles at The Globe. On television, Jude recently starred in the

UK version of Law & Order, Joe Penhall's Moses Jones and The #1 Ladies Detective
Agency (BBC). His long list of TV credits includes The Last Detective, Silent Witness,
Roger Roger, Land of Dreams, The Bill & Between the Lines. Film includes The
Tempest, Touched By A Stranger, Whisper the Way of the Child, Sahara and A
World Apart. Jude has also done extensive work for BBC Radio, including a long
run in the World Service's Westway.

Rob Compton Compeyson/Dance & Fight Captain
Rob trained at Arts Educational School. His theatre credits include:
Ghost of Christmas Past in A Christmas Carol for West Yorkshire
Playhouse and Christmas in New York at the Lyric, West End. Roles
whilst training include Friar Laurence in Romeo and Juliet - The Rock
Opera and Robbie Hart in The Wedding Singer.

Giles Cooper Herbert Pocket
Giles trained at the Central School of Speech and Drama.
His theatre credits include: After the Dance (National Theatre);
Dreams of Violence (Out of Joint/Soho Theatre); Think Global, F**k
Local (Out of Joint/Royal Court); Trilby (Finborough Theatre); The
Talented Mr Ripley (Northampton Theatre Royal); A Touch of the
Sun (Salisbury Playhouse); The Witches (Birmingham Rep and West
End); Full Circle (No.1 UK Tour/Triumph Entertainment); Twelfth Night
(Bolton Octagon); Across Oka & Rafts and Dreams (Manchester Royal Exchange).
His TV work includes Consenting Adults (BBC). Film work includes Apollo and The
Continents (Methodact) and The Nun (Filmax).

Russell Dixon Jaggers
Russell has just finished appearing in the West End in Flashdance –
The Musical at the Shaftesbury Theatre. He was a member of The
National Youth Theatre and trained at the Bristol Old Vic Theatre
School.

Theatre work includes: The Cardinal in The Duchess of Malfi,
Simonides in Pericles, Yeltsin in Moscow Gold (Royal Shakespeare
Company); Bergetto in 'Tis Pity She's A Whore, Cliff in A Small Family
Business, and more recently Chorus in Oedipus (National Theatre); A Chorus of
Disapproval (Lyric Theatre); The Glory Of The Garden (Duke Of York's); The Illustrious
Corpse (Soho Theatre); My Fair Lady (Cyprus and Denmark); On Your Toes (Royal

Festival Hall/Japan Tour); The Beggars Opera, The Magistrate, The Seagull, The Tempest (Royal Exchange Theatre, Manchester); A Christmas Carol (Birmingham Rep); Pacific Overtures, Follies, A Little Night Music (Leicester Haymarket); King Lear, Bouncers (Nottingham Playhouse); Who's Afraid of Virginia Wolf? (Sheffield Crucible); The Pillowman (Curve, Leicester); Equus, Waiting for Godot, The Importance of Being Earnest (Manchester Library Theatre); Cabaret, Masterclass (Derby Playhouse).

Film and television includes: The Vice, The Royal Today, Fat Friends, Heartbeat, Emmerdale (Yorkshire Television); The Grand, Coronation Street, Christmas Lights, Northern Lights, Eleventh Hour, See No Evil (Granada Television); Peak Practice, Kavanagh QC (Carlton TV); Faces Off (Radical Media UK); The Emperor's New Clothes (Bonaparte Films); Liam (Liam Films). He is a frequent broadcaster on Radios Three and Four.

Lynn Farleigh Miss Havisham

Lynn trained at Guildhall School of Music & Drama and has worked many times for the RSC and National Theatre, English Shakespeare Company and in the West End.

Recent theatre credits include: Solonika (West Yorkshire Playhouse); The Skin Game (Orange Tree, Richmond); Pravda (Chichester Festival Theatre); The Prince of Homburg (RSC/Lyric Hammersmith); The Family Reunion (RSC).

Television: Peep Show, Christmas Special (Channel 4); Sherlock (BBC); Casualty (BBC); Midsomer Murders (ITV); Wycliff (HTV); He Knew He Was Right (BBC); Pride and Prejudice (BBC). Feature Films: From Time To Time (FT2T Films); Miss Potter (Hopping Mad Productions). For Radio: Our Mutual Friend, Pickwick Papers, and Proust's Remembrance of Things Past.

Pooja Ghai Mrs Gargery/Molly

Pooja is a TV regular, playing Bushra in EastEnders and Tasmeen on BBC's Casualty.

Theatre work includes: Juganator by Titus Halder (Finborough Theatre); Stranger in my Kitchen, Bhena, Child's Play (Kali Theatre); Singh Tangoes (Kali Theatre/Tour/Riverside Studios); The Deranged Marriage, Where's My Desi Soulmate (Rifco); Meet the Mukherjees (Octagon Bolton); Rafta Rafta Tour (National Theatre); Last Chance (British Council Theatre, Bangladesh); Book Of The Banshee (National Tour/ Y. Arnaud/Pied Piper Theatre Co); Consequences (Tristan Bates Theatre); Unsung Lullaby (The Steam Industry); Female Of The Species (Global Cafe); Meena Dat-1999-2000, Lost For Words (Arc Theatre Ensemble); A Midsummer Night's Dream (Man in the Moon Theatre); Twelfth Night, Oedipus, Three Sisters (LAPA); Heroes (Blue Elephant Theatre); Tales From The Vienna Woods (The Gate Theatre); Metamorphosis (Burton-Taylor Theatre).

Other television includes: Doctors, Grease Monkeys II, Holby City (BBC); The Bill (ITV); Hyde and Sikh (BBC Talent). Pooja is also a regular voice on BBC Radio 3 and BBC Radio 4.

Shiv Grewal Pumblechook/A Public Speaker

Theatre includes: The Good Soul Of Szechuan (Young Vic); Rafta Rafta (National Theatre); Too Close To Home (Rasa/Manchester Library); A British Subject (E59E Theaters, Brits Off Broadway); Twelfth Night (Albany Theatre); 14 Songs 2 Weddings And A Funeral, Shaft Of Sunlight (Tamasha); Cafe Vesuvio (Manchester Royal Exchange); Far Away From England, A Midsummer Night's Dream, Just So Stories (London Bubble Theatre); A British Subject (The Pleasance, Edinburgh); A Streetcar Named Desire (Sherman Theatre); Balti Kings (West Yorkshire Playhouse); Behud by Gurpreet Kaur Bhatti, Gladiator Games (Theatre Royal Stratford East); Half Hearts - Quarter Measures, Taming of the Shrew (Avon Touring); Little Sister, Safar, (Made in Wales); Othello (Wales Actors Co); River on Fire, Strictly Dandia (Lyric, Hammersmith); Hawker, Women of the Dust (Bristol Old Vic); Zulu Hut Club (Derby Playhouse).

Shiv has extensive TV and Radio credits, including: Messiah III, Doctors, High Hopes, Holby City, Our Lady In Paris, Silver Street, The Liver Birds, Two Point Four Children (BBC Television); London's Burning (LWT), Slings & Arrows (Tiger Aspects), The Bill (Thames), The Last Enemy (ITV).

Simone James Estella
Simone trained at Rose Bruford.

Recent Theatre includes: Star Child (Almeida); Waiting (Purcell Rooms/Sadler's Wells); 365 (National Theatre of Scotland/Lyric, Hammersmith); Chatroom/Citizenship (National Theatre); Othello (Sam Wanamaker Festival).

Television includes regular appearances on EastEnders as Becca; Holby City, Silent Witness (BBC Television); Law and Order (ITV); Coming Up - Apples and Oranges (Channel 4).

Tony Jayawardena Joe Gargery
Television credits include: Moses Jones, Holby City, Doctors (all BBC); Trial And Retribution (La Plante Prods.); Blair (Mentorn Prods.); Hotel Babylon (Carnival Films).

Theatre credits include: Aslan in The Lion, The Witch And The Wardrobe (Northampton); London Assurance, All's Well That Ends Well and England People Very Nice (all National Theatre); Twelfth Night (RSC); Travels With My Aunt (Oldham Coliseum); A Fine Balance, Child Of The Divide (Tamasha); Jack And The Beanstalk (Barbican); Drive, Ride, Walk (Bridewell); Aladdin (Broadway); Behna (Kali/Soho Theatre); Jungle Book (Birmingham Stage Co.); Othello (Good Company).

Film credits include: Huge (Cinema 3 SPV2); A Bunch Of Amateurs (Trademark Films); Chasing Liberty (Alcon Entertainment).

Radio includes: Silverstreet (BBC).

Tariq Jordan Pip

Tariq, originally from Manchester, trained at The Webber Douglas Academy and Central School of Speech and Drama. His theatre credits include Fragile Land at Hampstead Theatre and Guantanamo at The Tricycle Theatre and the West End, including a performance at the House of Congress. His film credits include George Gently, Law and Order, Lewis, Shameless, Spooks and the Bafta award-winning BBC film White Girl. Tariq has just finished filming on the ITV drama Injustice.

Darren Kuppan Wemick

Theatre includes: We Love You City (Belgrade Theatre); Rafta, Rafta (Bolton Octagon/New Vic, Stoke); Aladdin (Theatre Royal Stratford East); East Is East (Birmingham Rep); Jamaica House (The Dukes Playhouse); Arabian Nights (New Vic, Stoke); Pretend You Have Big Buildings (The Royal Exchange); Bollywood Jane (West Yorkshire Playhouse).

Television includes: Spooks 8 (Spooks Ltd); Britannia High, The Adam & Shelly Show (Granada); Emmerdale (Yorkshire TV).

Radio includes: Divided We Fall (Mannmade Productions); The Prospect II (BBC Radio 4).

Kiran Landa Biddy

Kiran trained at the ITV Workshop.

Selected theatre credits: American Dream, Dark of the Moon, We Happy Few (ITV Workshop); Dov and Ali (Theatre 503); Arabian Nights (RSC).

Television: Wire In The Blood (Coastal Productions); 2:2 (BBC TV); Doctors (BBC TV) and Scott and Bailey (Scott & Bailey No2 Ltd for ITV).

Selected film credits: Shoot on Sight (Shoot on Sight); Song of the Holy Cow (Wellington Films); Curiosity (Dual Reality); True Meaning of Love (Fourmost Films).

Creative Team Biographies

Tanika Gupta Writer

Tanika Gupta was born and raised in London. Her first stage play, Voices on the Wind (1995) told the story of her 19-year-old great uncle, Dinesh Gupta, an Indian freedom fighter who was hanged by the British Raj as a terrorist in 1931.

Tanika has subsequently written many original stage plays, including: Skeleton (1997) Soho Theatre; an adaptation of Geeta Mehta's A River Sutra (Indoza 1997); The Waiting Room (2000) National Theatre; a translation of Brecht's The Good Woman of Setzuan (National Theatre Education 2001); Sanctuary (2002) National Theatre; and Inside Out (2002) for Clean Break. Her adaptation of Hobson's Choice (2003) played at the Young Vic; Fragile Land (2003) at Hampstead; and Gladiator Games (2005/6) at Sheffield Crucible and Theatre Royal Stratford East. Her play Sugar Mummies (2006) at the Royal Court Theatre, was followed by a group play, Catch (2006), co-written with four other women. Her most recent plays were Meet The Mukherjees (2008) at Bolton Octagon Theatre and White Boy (2007/8) for the National Youth Theatre at Soho Theatre.

Tanika has also written over 30 original radio plays for BBC Radio. She has written original dramas for television, including Bideshi (1996), Flight (1998) and Banglatown Banquet (2006, receiving a Prix Europa special commendation) as well as writing for EastEnders, Grange Hill and The Bill.

Tanika was awarded the John Whiting Award in 2000, the Asian Woman of Achievement Award in 2003 and the Amnesty International Award in 2005. She was also awarded an MBE for services to drama in 2008.

Nikolai Foster Director

Nikolai Foster was born in Copenhagen, Denmark and grew up in North Yorkshire. He trained at Drama Centre London and at the Crucible, Sheffield.

Foster has directed Shakespeare's Macbeth (Singapore Repretory Theatre); As You Like It (Grosvenor Park, Chester); Flashdance (Shaftesbury Theatre, London), an original musical by Tom Hedley, Robbie Roth & Robert Cary; two major revivals of plays by Noël Coward: Hay Fever (Chichester Festival Theatre) & A Song At Twilight (Mercury Theatre, Colchester, Theatre Royal Windsor and National Tour); Ayckbourn's Absent Friends (Oldham Coliseum/Harrogate Theatre); Bryony Lavery & Jason Carr's A Christmas Carol (West Yorkshire Playhouse, Leeds & Birmingham Rep); Barry Hines' Kes, adapted by Lawrence Till (Liverpool Playhouse & UK Tour); Dempsey and Rowe's The Witches of Eastwick (UK tour); Boucicault's London Assurance (Watermill Theatre, Newbury & UK Tour); Shaffer's Amadeus (Crucible, Sheffield); Andrew Lloyd Webber, Charles Hart & Don Black's Aspects of Love (UK National Tour & Nelson Mandela Theatre, South Africa); Orwell's Animal Farm, Louise Page's Salonika & Amanda Whittington's Bollywood Jane (West Yorkshire Playhouse, Leeds); Johnson's Dead Funny (Oldham Coliseum & National Tour); A Midsummer Night's Dream (Mercury Theatre, Colchester); Leoncavallo's Pagliacci (Pegasus Opera and English Touring Opera - National Tour); the Sondheim/Weidman musical play Assassins (Crucible, Sheffield); Ayckbourn's Season's

Greetings (Liverpool Playhouse); Steinbeck's Of Mice and Men (Mercury Theatre, Colchester); Williams' A Streetcar Named Desire (Clwyd Theatr Cymru); Corneille's The Liar - translated and adapted by Ranjit Bolt (Cochrane Theatre, London); and A Chorus Line (Crucible, Sheffield).

Nikolai has been director on attachment at the Sheffield Crucible, the Royal Court Theatre and National Theatre Studio.

http://web.mac.com/nikolaifoster

Colin Richmond Designer
Colin trained at the Royal Welsh College of Music and Drama, Cardiff and achieved a First Class BA Hons. Awards include: Lord Williams Design Award 2002 and 2003; and 2003 Linbury Prize Finalist. Colin became a Resident Designer as part of the Royal Shakespeare Company's Trainee Programme 2004-2005.

Colin's credits include: Entertaining Mr Sloane, Touched for the very first time, Ring Round The Moon, Bad Girls - The Musical, the RSC production of Breakfast With Mugabe (West End); Notes to Future Self, The Cherry Orchard, A Christmas Carol, Hapgood, The Bolt Hole, Low Dat (Birmingham Rep); Twelfth Night, Bollywood Jane, Salonika, Hapgood, Animal Farm, Billy Liar, A Christmas Carol (West Yorkshire Playhouse); L'Opera Seria (Italy); Hansel and Gretel (Northampton Theatre Royal); Play/Not I (BAC); Human Rites (Old Southwark Playhouse); House Of The Gods!, Letters of a Love Betrayed (Music Theatre Wales/Royal Opera House 2/National Tour); Restoration (Bristol Old Vic, Headlong Theatre); The Shadow Of A Gunman (Glasgow Citizens); Hansel & Gretel, Sondheim's Sweeney Todd - TMA Best Musical Production 2010; The Firebird (Dundee Rep Theatre); Suddenly Last Summer (Theatr Clwyd); Europe (Barbican); Absent Friends (Oldham Coliseum); The May Queen (Liverpool Everyman); Amadeus (Sheffield Crucible); All the Fun of The Fair (Number 1 National Tour); When We Are Married (West Yorkshire Playhouse/ Liverpool Playhouse); La Bohème, Don Pasquale (Holland Park Opera); The Lady in the Van (Salisbury Playhouse); The Caucasian Chalk Circle (Shared Experience/ West Yorkshire Playhouse/Nottingham Playhouse); The Three Musketeers and The Princess of Spain (English Touring Theatre/Traverse/Belgrade Theatre Coventry)

Television credits include: first series and pre-production assistant designer on Doctor Who (BBC Wales)

Lee Curran Lighting Designer
Lee has been a lighting designer for over 10 years. Working primarily in contemporary dance, he has created designs for artists and companies including Rambert, CandoCo, The Gate Theatre, Jonathan Burrows, Mark Baldwin, Nick Cave, Rafael Bonachela, Darren Ellis, Probe, and Iain Forsyth & Jane Pollard. Most notably, Lee has collaborated with Hofesh Shechter on four pieces for his internationally acclaimed company, including the 2008 Critics Circle Award winner In Your Rooms, and South Bank Show Award 2011 nominee Political Mother. Lee is also Head of Technical at the ICA in London.

www.leecurran.net

Nicki Wells Composer

Emerging new singer/songwriter/composer, 22 year old Nicki Wells, having just gained a first class honours degree in music, has been working on her debut album as well as multiple collaborations with artists and producers including the acclaimed Nitin Sawhney. She has already been featured on his work ranging from album recordings to performances with Akram Khan and the Royal Opera House.

Having already performed as a singer to sell out audiences in regions as diverse as Australia, the Middle East, the Far East & Europe, she has astounded audiences the world over with her incomparable ability to traverse the gaps between old and new, east and west and contemporary chic and classicism. Nicki is due to perform with Nitin Sawhney at the Royal Albert Hall on May 6th of this year before a forthcoming tour of America, and is featured on the current BBC hit series the Human Planet.

Sebastian Frost Sound Designer

Sebastian's theatre designs include Anthony & Cleopatra (Liverpool Playhouse); Little Shop Of Horrors (Birmingham Rep); Riff Raff (Arcola); A Christmas Carol (West Yorkshire Playhouse/Birmingham Rep); The Pros, Cons & A Screw (Derby); All The Fun Of The Fair (Garrick & UK tour); The Common Pursuit, Take Flight, Total Eclipse (Menier); The Glass Menagerie (Apollo); Sunday In The Park With George (Menier/Wyndhams); Carnival (Venice); Trainspotting (UK Tour); Tonight's The Night (Victoria Palace); Bomb-itty Of Errors (New Ambassadors); Mysteries (Queens); Boy Band (Gielgud); Kat And The Kings (Broadway/Vaudeville); Summer Begins (Donmar); Colour Of Justice (Victoria Palace); Fame (UK Tour) and What The Butler Saw (Bath). In 2008 he received the first ever Best Sound Design of a Musical Tony Award nomination for Sunday In The Park With George on Broadway.

Other work includes International Motorshows for Ford Motor Company; exhibitions for Star Trek (Hyde Park); Thunderbirds Are Go (NEC); Sony (Earls Court); and installations for Disney, Harrods, Harry Potter and Coca Cola, Lumiere (Durham); and the Queen's Golden Jubilee celebrations.

Zoobin Surty Movement and Choreographer

Zoobin Surty is a Zorastrian dance artist from Mumbai, India, trained in Indian classical forms of dance. Zoobin is a graduate of the Northern School of Contemporary Dance and is a Cultural Dance Ambassador/resident artist from South Asian Arts in Leeds.

His expertise and experience in Contemporary Bollywood dance has been in demand worldwide. He has performed, choreographed and directed dance theatre, commercials, pop stars, films with his dance company and has toured India, USA, Canada, South Africa, Dubai & Japan.

In 2007 he choreographed Bollywood Jane for West Yorkshire Playhouse and his new dance work Dukh-sukh toured in March 2008, soon followed by a new choreography, mentored by Keran Virdee, Saa-uk and CYC.

Cressida Carré Movement

Cressida's credits include: Wind In The Willows (Derby Live); Cinderella (Devonshire Park Theatre); Departure Lounge (Waterloo East Theatre); Elegies For Angels, Punks and Raging Queens (Black Box, Belfast); A...My Name Is Alice (New Players Theatre); A Chorus Line (BAC); Jack And The Beanstalk (Theatre Royal, Bury St Edmunds); Steel Pier (Chelsea Theatre); The Fix (Albany Theatre); Into The Woods (Greenwich Theatre); Before The Night Is Through (Millfield Theatre); Dick Whittington (Harlow Playhouse); Closer Than Ever (Chelsea Theatre); Blues Brothers Unlimited (Centrepoint Theatre, Dubai); The Witches Of Eastwick (Albany Theatre); Hot Mikado (Chelsea Theatre); Have A Nice Life (Edinburgh Festival); West Side Story (BAC); Lucky Stiff (New Wimbledon Studio Theatre); The Diary Of Me (Harlow Playhouse); Passage Of Dreams (Bridewell Theatre); Godspell (BAC); Jesus Christ Superstar (Kings Theatre, Portsmouth); Espresso Trasho (Arts Theatre); Dorian (Greenwich Theatre); The Clearing (Tramway Theatre, Glasgow).

Nicola Samer Associate Director

Nicola was born in Sydney, Australia and gained her MA Theatre Directing in London (Middlesex University). Training: Russian Academy of Dramatic Arts (Moscow), Directors' Lab 2010 Lincoln Centre Theatre (New York), directing at the National Institute of Dramatic Arts (Sydney) and working on attachment with the Royal Opera House (London).

Directing credits include: Fiddler On The Roof (Cambridge Arts Theatre); The 52 Show (Leicester Square Theatre); Who Are Our New Friends? (Theatre Lab); Can I Get A Kiss From Daisy? (Old Vic, reading); Miss Julie (Sterts Theatre, Cornwall); Scenes Of A Massacre (Pilot, Birmingham); The Last Days Of Empire (Pleasance, London); The Tempest (New Theatre, Sydney) and Jew! A Musical (Lost Theatre Festival, London).

Other credits include: Associate Director - Flashdance (West End); My Fair Lady (Bronowski Productions, Plenary Hall, Malaysia); Children's Director - Kes (Liverpool Everyman Playhouse); Resident Director - UK tours of Aspects Of Love and The Witches Of Eastwick; Don Giovanni (Hampstead Garden Opera); Follies (London Palladium); My Fair Lady (The Esplanade, Singapore); Dancing at Lughnasa (New Theatre, Sydney); Benda's Romeo & Juliet (Bampton Classical Opera, UK Tour); Assistant Director - Sound of Music (UK Tour); Eugene Onegin (British Youth Opera, Peacock Theatre) and A Family Affair (Arcola Theatre). Nicola is co-founder of IronBark, presenting Australian Theatre in the UK.

Kate Waters Fight Director

Kate is one of only two women on the Equity Register of Fight Directors and works regularly in regional theatre all over the country as well as at the National Theatre and in the West End.

Recent work includes: Frankenstein, Seasons Greetings, Hamlet, Twelfth Night, Women Beware Women & Warhorse (National Theatre); Othello (West Yorkshire Playhouse and West End); King Lear (RSC); Spring Awakening, The Musical (Lyric and West End); Entertaining Mr Sloane (West End); Widowers Houses (Manchester Royal Exchange); The Count of Monte Cristo & Bedroom Farce (West Yorkshire Playhouse); The Lion, The Witch & The Wardrobe (Birmingham Rep); A Midsummer Night's Dream (Rose Theatre); The Pride (Royal Court); How the Other Half Loves (Stephen Joseph Theatre); Kes & Tis Pity She's A Whore (Liverpool Everyman/Playhouse); As You Like It (Watford Palace) and Hamlet (Shakespeare @ the Tobacco Factory, Bristol) directed by Jonathan Miller.

Kay Magson CDG Casting Director

Kay's theatre credits include: The Solid Gold Cadillac (Garrick); Dangerous Corner (West Yorkshire Playhouse/West End); Round the Horne… Revisited, Dracula (National tours); Singin' in the Rain (West Yorkshire Playhouse, NT/National tour); Aspects of Love, All The Fun of the Fair and The Witches of Eastwick (National tours); Kes (Liverpool and National tour); Sweeney Todd (Royal Festival Hall).

Kay was resident at the West Yorkshire Playhouse for 17 years where she cast many shows including Hamlet, The McKellen Ensemble Season, the Patrick Stewart Priestley Season and many others. She also casts regularly for Salisbury Playhouse, Northampton Theatres (including the Young America season which transferred to the National); Liverpool Everyman and Playhouse, Hull Truck and the Manchester Library Theatre.

She is currently working on Walk Like a Panther, a pilot TV for Finite Films.

Kay is a member of the Casting Director's Guild of Great Britain (CDG).

Watford Palace Theatre...
is a local theatre with a national reputation.

The creative hub at the heart of Watford, the Palace engages people through commissioning, creating and presenting high-quality theatre, and developing audiences, artists and communities through exciting opportunities to participate.

Contributing to the identity of Watford and Hertfordshire, the Palace enriches people's lives, increases pride in the town, and raises the profile of the area through its work.

The quality of work on stage and beyond is central to the Theatre's ethos. Recently the Palace has enjoyed critical acclaim for its productions of Gary Owen's **Mrs Reynolds and The Ruffian** commissioned by the Palace (2010), Neil Simon's **Brighton Beach Memoirs** (2010) and Charlotte Keatley's **My Mother Said I Never Should** (2009). The Theatre's busy 2011 programme includes a major revival of Ayckbourn's **Time of My Life** directed by Artistic Director Brigid Larmour, and a new play by Julian Mitchell, **Family Business**.

Community partnerships have led to the success of projects such as **Windrush** (2010), **Hello, Mister Capello** (2010) and **Milestones** (2008), all of which have brought together the creativity of Watford's diverse local communities. These build on the year-round programme of Palace and Hertfordshire County Youth Theatres, adult workshops, backstage tours, community choir and extensive work with local schools.

The beautiful 600-seat Edwardian Palace Theatre is a Grade II listed building. Refurbished in 2004, the Theatre offers modern and accessible facilities including its own rehearsal room, wardrobe and scenic workshop. Recently the Theatre opened a new Green Room Bar, refurbished its Cafe and Foyer and continues to develop the quality of experience for the tens of thousands of people visiting the Theatre each year.

A year in numbers...
- Reaching a total of 150,000 people
- Over 16,000 participatory sessions
- A season brochure goes to 80,000 customers
- 115,000 unique website visits
- A pantomime attended by over 25,000 visitors
- Visits generate over £1m of spending in the local economy
- Over 250 performances
- More than a dozen productions produced or co-produced

And in 2011 Watford Palace will be bolder than ever...
- Presenting internationally acclaimed outdoor theatre in Watford Town Centre
- Introducing a curated programme of 250+ film screenings
- Refurbishing the Theatre's Edwardian Facade to its former glory
- Celebrating local diversity through a programme of cultural celebrations
- Welcoming Rifco Arts as a Resident Company based at the Theatre

ETT
ENGLISH
TOURING
THEATRE

surprise • delight • enrich • engage

Under the directorship of Rachel Tackley, **ETT** presents potent, vivid and vital productions of new and classic plays to audiences far and wide. An award-winning powerhouse of touring theatre, **ETT** works with a rich and varied mix of the country's leading directors, actors and artists to stage thrilling and ambitious theatre that is vigorous, popular and, above all, entertaining.

Producer of the Year 2010

From Edinburgh to Exeter, and Sheffield to Southampton — in 2010 we gave 223 performances in 22 venues all over the country — look out for us in your region in 2011!

ett.org.uk

Supported by
**ARTS COUNCIL
ENGLAND**

**BRITISH
COUNCIL**

Photographs by Robert Day and Manuel Harlan

Work created at and with Watford Palace Theatre regularly tours nationally. Productions you may have seen recently include:

Watford Palace Theatre
ON TOUR

Great Expectations
by Charles Dickens, adapted by Tanika Gupta, co-produced with English Touring Theatre

Songs From A Hotel Bedroom
by Kate Flatt and Peter Rowe, music by Kurt Weill, co-produced with Segue and the New Wolsey Theatre and co-commissioned by ROH2 at the Royal Opera House

The Human Comedy
from an original story by William Saroyan, book by William Dumaresq with music by Galt MacDermot, co-produced with the Young Vic and The Opera Group

Von Ribbentrop's Watch
a new play by Laurence Marks and Maurice Gran, co-produced with Oxford Playhouse

Bunny
by Jack Thorne, a Fringe First-winning production in association with nabokov and the Mercury Colchester

Stickman
from the book by Julia Donaldson, co-produced with Scamp, which has toured internationally and played at London's Soho Theatre and the Edinburgh Festival

My Hamlet with Linda Marlowe
an international partnership led by the Palace and NFA International Arts and Culture with Fingers Theatre, Tbilisi

The Lion's Face
a new opera from poet Glyn Maxwell and composer Elena Langer, co-produced with The Opera Group and Brighton Dome & Festival

Soul Play
a new piece of dance theatre co-produced with Kate Flatt projects

2nd May 1997
by Jack Thorne, co-produced with nabokov and the Bush Theatre in association with the Mercury Colchester

Street Scene
Music by Kurt Weill, book by Elmer Rice, lyrics by Langston Hughes, co-produced with The Opera Group and the Young Vic, which won the Evening Standard award for Best Musical

Tintin
the stage adaptation, co-produced with the Young Vic, which toured nationally before transferring to the West End

To keep in touch with Watford Palace's work both on the Watford stage and through national touring, sign up to our Twitter Feed or Facebook Page

www.watfordpalacetheatre.co.uk

For Watford Palace Theatre

Follow us:

Supported by
ARTS COUNCIL ENGLAND

GREAT EXPECTATIONS

First published in 2011 by Oberon Books Ltd
521 Caledonian Road, London N7 9RH
Tel: 020 7607 3637 / Fax: 020 7607 3629
e-mail: info@oberonbooks.com
www.oberonbooks.com

A catalogue record for this book is available from the British Library.

ISBN: 978-1-84943-122-4

Cover image by Jorge Royan / Alamy

Printed in Great Britain by CPI Antony Rowe, Chippenham.

Charles Dickens

GREAT EXPECTATIONS

Adapted for the stage by Tanika Gupta

OBERON BOOKS
LONDON

Characters

PIP
Indian youth – ages from 12/13 years old to 25.

MAGWITCH
Black/African Convict from the Cape Colony
(Cape Town – South Africa).

CONVICT aka COMPEYSON
'Young man' vicious convict/Miss Havisham's lover. English.

JOE GARGERY
Pip's brother-in-law.

MRS GARGERY
Pip's older sister.

MR PUMBLECHOOK
Village Priest.

BIDDY
Family friend of Pip's. Indian village girl.
12/13 – 25. Later marries Joe.

MISS HAVISHAM
Elderly English woman.

ESTELLA
Ages from 12/13 years old to 25.
Mixed race (African/Indian) beauty.

HERBERT POCKET
Ages from 12/13 years old to 25. English young man.

JAGGERS
English lawyer practicing in Calcutta. Rogue
with a conscience.

WEMICK
Jaggers' clerk. Indian working class.

The play is set in India circa 1861

Other characters in the Ensemble

PIP'S VILLAGERS

2 X SOLDIERS HUNTING CONVICTS

PEOPLE IN THE STREETS OF CALCUTTA

MOLLY

PUBLIC SPEAKER

ACT I

SCENE 1

India circa 1861.

It is the end of the day and dusk is falling. We are in the deserted cremation ground – outdoors on the banks of the river with a ghat that goes down to the river. There are piles of wood stacked ready for a pyre, human skulls scattered on the floor and a small shrine to the Goddess Kali sat in pride of place. A funeral pyre is still smoking and the overall atmosphere is foreboding. PIP, a 12/13 year old boy, enters. He is shabbily dressed and carrying a stick. He looks fearful as he wanders into the cremation grounds. PIP pokes the funeral pyre absent-mindedly with his stick and looks around him afraid. He approaches one of the skulls and stares hard at it. Dark shadows creep around him and the little boy looks terrified.

PIP starts to cry and a voice booms from the darkness of the water.

MAGWITCH: Hold your noise!

PIP jumps and tries to run but a large African man, dressed in ragged convict's garb limps out from the river, dripping with water, looking like a sea monster. He grabs PIP and holds him fast.

MAGWITCH: Keep still – devil, or I'll cut your throat!

MAGWITCH is a terrifying looking man and he looms large over the boy. He is still wearing leg irons and is covered in bruises and dirt. His feet are bare and his leg is bloodied where the leg irons have dug into his skin.

PIP: Oh! Don't cut my throat sir. Don't!

MAGWITCH: Name. Quick!

PIP: Pip.

MAGWITCH: Again. Louder!

PIP: Pip. Pip.

MAGWITCH: Show me where you are living. The place… point!

PIP raises a shaky hand and points in the direction of his house in the distance. MAGWITCH follows the direction of PIP's hand and then effortlessly lifts PIP up and turns him upside down. He shakes him. Some fruit falls out of his pockets. MAGWITCH places PIP high up on a stack of wood and eats the fruit ravenously. He keeps a close eye on PIP though who sits and shakes with fear.

MAGWITCH: What fat cheeks… like mangoes I could eat them.

MAGWITCH cruelly pinches PIP's cheeks and makes munching sounds.

PIP: Please don't.

MAGWITCH: Your mother?

PIP points towards the river. MAGWITCH swivels around, half expecting to see a woman, suddenly terrified and ready to bolt.

PIP: There. In the river.

MAGWITCH peers out into the darkness.

MAGWITCH: River?

PIP: And my father. We scattered their ashes there.

MAGWITCH: Ahhh…you're an orphan boy?

PIP: Yes sir.

MAGWITCH: Who are you living with ? Supposing I allow you to live – which I haven't decided yet?

PIP: My sister sir, Mrs Gargery.

MAGWITCH: Just you and your sister, on your own?

PIP: No….sir…she's the wife of Joe Gargery, the village cobbler sir.

MAGWITCH: Cobbler, eh?

MAGWITCH looks down at his leg irons and looks thoughtful.

PIP shakes. MAGWITCH snaps his attention back to PIP.

MAGWITCH: Why're you staring at me like that?

PIP: Sorry sir.

MAGWITCH: Trying to commit my face to your memory are you?

PIP: No sir…I never seen a ..a…

MAGWITCH: A black man?

PIP shakes his head and looks away.

MAGWITCH: Stick out in a crowd I do.

I've seen Indians as black as me though. Take her for example.

MAGWITCH cocks his head in the direction of the Goddess Kali.

MAGWITCH: Now, she's my kind've Goddess.

Suddenly MAGWITCH grabs PIP by the scruff and tilts him back.

MAGWITCH: I am thinking about whether or not I should let you live. How old are you?

PIP: Twelve years old sir.

MAGWITCH: You know what a file is?

PIP: Yes sir.

MAGWITCH: And rice?

PIP: Yes sir.

MAGWITCH: You get me a file and you get me some rice.

PIP is clinging to MAGWITCH as he tilts him back so far. PIP nearly falls.

PIP: Feeling sick…oh…please!

MAGWITCH gives PIP another jab but then catches him before he falls off the pile of wood completely.

MAGWITCH: Tomorrow morning early, that file and some rice. Don't you dare say a word or dare to make a sign concerning you seeing me and you'll be allowed to live. You fail me or you go from my words in any particular, no matter how small it is and …

MAGWITCH makes a ripping gesture at PIP's chest.

PIP whimpers.

MAGWITCH: I am not alone. There's a man hiding with me, in comparison with which man, I am an Angel. He obeys me. That man has a secret way peculiar to himself of getting at a boy, and at his heart and at his liver.

PIP: Oh!

MAGWITCH: A boy may be warm in bed, may be thinking himself comfortable and safe, but that man will softly be creeping and creeping his way to him and tearing him open. I am keeping that young man from harming you at the present moment, with great difficulty.

PIP: I promise!

MAGWITCH: You swear?

PIP: I'll bring the file and the rice to you…first thing.

MAGWITCH picks up PIP again and roughly carries him to the shrine of Kali. He forces PIP to kneel before the shrine, pushing him down.

MAGWITCH: Say… Kali strike you dead if you don't?

PIP: Kali strike me dead if I don't do as I am asked.

MAGWITCH: And dance on my cold dead bones.

PIP: And…and…

MAGWITCH: Say it!

PIP: And dance on my cold dead bones.

MAGWITCH walks away.

MAGWITCH: Remember… your promise… and you remember that man!

PIP: Goo-goo-night sir.

PIP does an elaborate namasté but MAGWITCH ignores him. Instead, he limps away, past the smoking pyre and into the night.

PIP watches MAGWITCH, rooted to the spot in fear for some time before exiting sharply.

SCENE 2

We are in an Indian village, again by the river banks but further away from the crematorium. JOE, an Indian man in his late twenties is a cobbler by trade and he works from his small mud hut which is also his and PIP's home. Dressed in a lunghi (Indian sarong) and bare chested, he looks big and strong but has a mildness to his manner. Dead hens hang upside down from a wire in front of the hut. JOE is surrounded by leather bags, sandals, etc. PIP creeps in behind him and steals a couple of the hens hanging up. He stuffs them unseen into a sack and stashes them under some sacks of rice. Then PIP approaches JOE.

JOE: Your **Didi's* been out a dozen times looking for you Pip. She's on the warpath.

PIP: Is she?

JOE: What's worse, is that she's got Tickler with her.

PIP looks distressed.

She made a grab at Tickler and she rampaged out. That's what she did. She rampaged out Pip.

PIP: Has she been gone long Joe?

*Didi – Bengali term for older sister

27

MRS GARGERY: *(Off.)* Pip! Pip? Is that you?

PUMBLECHOOK: *(Off.)* There he is! I can see him.

JOE: *(Urgent.)* Hide… Get behind me and get something down the back of you.

JOE quickly hands PIP a towel which PIP shoves down the back of his trousers. MRS GARGERY enters followed closely by PUMBLECHOOK, the village Priest. She is furious as she brandishes her cane 'TICKLER'. PIP runs around, trying to avoid her. PUMBLECHOOK tries to help her, whilst JOE tries to protect PIP.

MRS GARGERY: Where have you been, you monkey? Tell me what you've been doing to wear me away with fright and worry?

PIP: Only been to the Crematorium.

MRS GARGERY: Crematorium? That dirty, filthy place?

PUMBLECHOOK: It's only fit for untouchables!

MRS GARGERY: What were you doing there? If it wasn't for me you'd have been to the crematorium long ago and stayed there. Who brought you up by hand?

PIP: You did.

MRS GARGERY: And why did I do it?

PIP: I don't know.

MRS GARGERY: *I* don't either. I'd never do it again! It's bad enough being a cobbler's wife without being your sister. Come here now, and take your punishment.

PUMBLECHOOK: If it wasn't for your good sister taking pity on you, you would have been destitute.

MRS GARGERY: Thank you for reminding him Uncle.
The boy doesn't appreciate his good fortune or family honour.

PUMBLECHOOK: He has been the world of trouble to you.

MRS GARGERY: Trouble? Trouble! He's had every childhood illness you can have, fevers, convulsions, stomach cramps and each time, who had to nurse him? Who had to fork out to buy the medicine? Why, once he even jumped from the top branches of the guava tree and nearly broke both his legs.

PUMBLECHOOK: Would have served him right if he did.

MRS GARGERY: Why is it that the young are never grateful?

PUMBLECHOOK: Naturally vicious.

MRS GARGERY: True! The sacrifices I've made for that boy. It's my *karma*. I must have done something terrible in my past life to be rewarded with such an ungrateful wretch.

All through this tirade, JOE surreptitiously protects PIP but gets a few thwacks in doing so. Eventually, PUMBLECHOOK manages to grab PIP, pull him out from behind JOE. MRS GARGERY whacks him a few times with her cane. There is a boom of canon fire in the distance. Everyone stops and looks up.

JOE: There's another convict off.

PIP uses this opportunity to hide behind JOE.

JOE: There was an escaped convict last night, after sunset. I heard the warning shot. Looks like they're firing another warning.

MRS GARGERY: That'll be two convicts running out there in the marshes. It'll be a miracle if we're not all murdered in our beds tonight.

MRS GARGERY suddenly notices her hens.

Oh Look! One of my chickens has gone!

PUMBLECHOOK: And you work so hard to put food in this boy's mouth. You hear that, boy? From morning 'til night, she slaves away for you.

MRS GARGERY: *(Suddenly frightened.)* Convicts? Not here?

Surely!

MRS GARGERY gasps.

MR PUMBLECHOOK: Bandits in the village – imagine!

JOE stands over PIP, quietly protecting him.

PIP: What's a convict Joe?

PUMBLECHOOK: What a questioner he is.

PIP: *Didi* I should like to know – if you wouldn't mind – where the firing comes from?

MRS GARGERY: From the Hulks!

PIP: And please, what's Hulks?

MRS GARGERY: That's the way with this boy. Answer him one question and he'll ask you a dozen directly. Hulks are prison ships from the city.

JOE: When I was little, and I saw those Hulks from the shore, they used to scare me. Big and black, like ghost ships, you can hear grown men moaning from inside. Ugly things they are. Cribbed and barred and covered in massive rusty chains just like the prisoners

PIP: And who gets put into prison ships?

MRS GARGERY: You and your questions!

PUMBLECHOOK: People are put into Hulks because they do murder and because they rob and do all sorts of bad: and they always begin by asking questions.

JOE: The Hulks take the convicts to Andaman. Once you're on that island, there's no escape.

PUMBLECHOOK: An island full of human flesh eating savages.

PIP looks afraid.

PIP: And these convicts… they're really bad people?

PUMBLECHOOK: More questions!

JOE: I think there are many of them that aren't that bad but the English say they are.

PUMBLECHOOK: They're trouble makers that's for sure.

JOE: And some of them were in the wrong place at the wrong time.

MRS GARGERY: Don't fill his head with rubbish Mr Gargery.

MR PUMBLECHOOK: They're a danger to us. Jump ship and follow the river bank down stream. Takes them straight to our little village on the way to the city. It's not as safe round here as it used to be.

PUMBLECHOOK: If you ever bump into one of these convicts, remember, they are demons, devil worshippers and murderers. You run boy, run away as fast as your legs will carry you.

MRS GARGERY: Hey! Where are your manners boy! Pip!

(Calls out.) Come back here at once! Pip!

JOE watches as PIP disappears. MRS GARGERY is furious.

JOE shakes his head,

JOE: I'll get him. All that talk of convicts frightened him.

PUMBLECHOOK: He was the one who kept asking questions.

MRS GARGERY: And that's what you get when you're too inquisitive.

JOE looks at PUMBLECHOOK and MRS GARGERY and exits wordlessly.

SCENE 3

It is lighter now and the sun is up. PIP enters the crematorium with a small sack. A dead body which has been covered by a cloth is lying on a stretcher by a pile of wood. PIP eyes the corpse with fear and then spots the convict sat on the ground, head lolling as he dozes. PIP approaches him gingerly and taps the convict who jumps up.

CONVICT: What the hell do you want...little bastard...?

PIP is taken by surprise and realises that this is a different convict to the one he met. He wears the same convict clothes and is dirty and ragged but he is English. The CONVICT makes a swipe at him but he is obviously weak.

CONVICT: Savage! Ragamuffin!

The English CONVICT staggers to his feet. He blinks in the sunlight and looks dazed.

PIP: Sorry sir.

CONVICT: *(Well spoken.)* Get away from me. Get away I say! Stop gawking at me.

PIP: I...I thought you were the other convict.

CONVICT: What other convict?

PIP: I don't know his name but...

CONVICT: Is he nearby?

PIP: He asked me to come and meet him here...

CONVICT: When did you last see him?

PIP: Yesterday.

CONVICT: Was he a black man? The other convict? Tell me!

PIP nods. The CONVICT looks afraid.

CONVICT: Get away from here, before he comes back.

Get away!

CONVICT bolts and runs away.

PIP looks afraid but settles down to wait for MAGWITCH. Eventually MAGWITCH arrives. PIP hurriedly takes the food out of his bundles and empties his pocket of fruit, etc. MAGWITCH unfolds a packet of bamboo leaves and starts to gobble the rice. He eyes the urn.

PIP: **Tari,* Joe makes it.

MAGWITCH grabs the urn and drinks it back. He coughs slightly.

PIP watches MAGWITCH wolfing down the food. MAGWITCH keeps peering out around him, listening to the sounds. He stops suddenly to listen at the sound of some distant animals.

MAGWITCH: You haven't been lying to me? Haven't brought anyone with you?

PIP: No sir!

MAGWITCH: Haven't been telling anyone about me?

PIP: No.

MAGWITCH: I believe you. You'd be a cruel young thing if you could be helping to hunt a wretched animal like me.

MAGWITCH digs around in the sack and finds a whole chicken, cooked. He rips it apart and gobbles more.

MAGWITCH: Delicious. Your sister's a good cook.

PIP look embarrassed.

PIP: I cooked it sir. For you.

MAGWITCH stops and looks at PIP surprised.

MAGWITCH offers PIP a small piece of chicken. PIP hesitates.

MAGWITCH: Go on.

PIP takes the chicken and nibbles daintily.

PIP: I'm glad you're enjoying your food.

* *Tari – A strong alcoholic drink made from fermented rice.*

MAGWITCH: What?

PIP: I said I'm glad you're enjoying your food.

MAGWITCH looks at PIP surprised.

MAGWITCH: Thank you my boy. I do.

PIP: Where are you from sir?

MAGWITCH: Meaning?

PIP: Are you from another country?

MAGWITCH: Yes. Africa. Heard of it?

PIP: Yes. Where they have giraffes?

MAGWITCH: Very good. Go to school do you?

PIP shakes his head.

MAGWITCH: You can read and write though?

PIP: A bit.

MAGWITCH: Take it from me. Learn your letters…only way forward.

PIP: What country in Africa?

MAGWITCH: What country he asks me?! Cape Colony – at the very tip of Africa. Lions and hippos there too.

PIP: I should like to go there one day and see for myself.

MAGWITCH: It's a beautiful place, but not a place to visit whilst those white locusts are sweeping through the land.

PIP: Aren't they all the same colour as you there?

MAGWITCH: Not anymore. It's like here, only nastier.

PIP: Begging your pardon sir. How did you end up in this country? Speaking our tongue?

MAGWITCH: Came as a young man as a sailor. Crossed those oceans many times – went as far as China. Settled here and called it home. But everywhere those white devils treat the black man worse than the brown man.

PIP watches MAGWITCH eat, gobble, look side to side as if someone is about to take his food away.

MAGWITCH: What're you staring at now boy?

PIP: Sorry sir, but you look like a dog eating, snapping up your food like that.

MAGWITCH looks at PIP, annoyed at first and then he laughs heartily.

MAGWITCH: Little child. Little boy. A dog he says!

MAGWITCH laughs some more and then woofs like a dog. PIP almost smiles.

PIP: I can't really get any more food for you and you haven't saved any for him.

MAGWITCH: Him? Who's 'him'?

PIP: The young man you talked about. That was hidden with you.

MAGWITCH: Oh ah! *(He laughs.)* Yes, yes! He won't be needing any food.

PIP: He looked as though he did.

MAGWITCH: Looked? When?

PIP: Just now…I found him nodding asleep and thought it was you.

MAGWITCH grabs hold of PIP and stares at him hard. PIP looks terrified again.

PIP: Dressed like you, you know and…and…with the same reason for wanting to borrow a file. Didn't you hear the canon last night?

MAGWITCH: Then there *was* firing.

PIP: I thought you would've heard it. It was very loud.

MAGWITCH lets go of PIP.

MAGWITCH: When a man is out there on the marshes, alone, desperate and starving, he hears nothing all night, but guns firing and voices calling. He sees the soldiers with their red coats lighted up by the torches closing in on him. Hears his number called, hears himself challenged, hears the rattle of the muskets, hears the orders: "Make ready! Present! Cover him Steady men!" And then he realises there's nothing...this man, did you notice anything about him?

PIP: He had a badly bruised face.

MAGWITCH: Here?

MAGWITCH strikes the side of his face. PIP nods.

MAGWITCH: Which way did he run?

MAGWITCH crams the rest of the food that's left into his pockets and the sack. He makes as if he's going to run.

MAGWITCH: Show me the way boy. I'll sniff him out like a blood hound.

PIP points in the direction the CONVICT ran off. MAGWITCH limps forward but then cries out in pain.

MAGWITCH: Aaghhh...curses on this iron...my sore leg!

PIP picks up the file off the ground and hands it to MAGWITCH. MAGWITCH dumps the sack and gets down and starts furiously filing at his leg iron. PIP watches him for a while and then slowly backs away.

MAGWITCH: *(Mutters under his breath.)* My leg...get this bloody thing off...come on come on...

PIP: I have to go.
Sir?

MAGWITCH ignores PIP and continues filing at his leg iron.

MAGWITCH: Like animals…chained up like a dog on a leash… curse them…curse this iron…bloody English bastards… string us all up if they could…

PIP watches a while longer and then quickly runs away. MAGWITCH doesn't even notice he's gone.

SCENE 4

Crematorium. Kali Pooja.

It is night time. A dhol player leads a procession into the crematorium. The Goddess Kali is brought forward and garlanded with blood red strings of flowers.The village are having a celebration/ pooja to Kali. PUMBLECHOOK, JOE, MRS GARGERY and PIP are all there. We also see BIDDY, a young Indian girl of the village. She stands close to PIP. Conch shells blare. It is a colourful and loud spectacle. PIP is lighting some lamps.

MRS GARGERY: Hurry up will you boy!

BIDDY runs forward and helps PIP to light the last of the lamps and then watch JOE dancing to the dhol. He laughs and claps. JOE drags PIP and BIDDY in to dance with him. They are interrupted suddenly by loud shouting and cursing.

MAGWITCH: *(Off.)* I'll teach you a lesson…you'll burn in the fires of hell! Lying, filthy, treacherous….

CONVICT comes rushing through, chased by MAGWITCH. They are both bruised, bloodied and even wilder looking than before. Everyone hushes. The pooja comes to an abrupt end.

MAGWITCH: I'll tear you limb from limb, I'll rip your insides out and feed them to the dogs…!

Two uniformed soldiers rush in carrying muskets.

SERGEANT: Stand back everyone!

SOLDIER 1: Convicts! Runaways!

JOE grabs hold of PIP and BIDDY pulls them back to protect them.

PUMBLECHOOK hides behind the statue of Kali.

SERGEANT: *(Calls out.)* Surrender you wretches!

The SOLDIERS take aim with their muskets and point at the convicts.

SERGEANT: *(Calls out.)* There's no way out of here!

MAGWITCH chases CONVICT and the two fight. The SOLDIERS continue to point their rifles at the men. MAGWITCH tries to strangle the CONVICT.

MAGWITCH: You will go straight to hell... Like Satan's serpent...think you can get the better of me?

CONVICT: Help! Help!

SERGEANT: Surrender you two!

CONVICT: He's trying to murder me!

MAGWITCH: If I wanted to murder you, I wouldn't be *trying* – I would *do* it!

The SERGEANT fires a warning rifle shot. The crowd scream and cower for cover. MAGWITCH suddenly stops fighting and pulls up the CONVICT by the scruff of his neck, hauls him up and throws the CONVICT at their feet.

MAGWITCH: There, he's all yours. But watch him.

The SOLDIERS grab them both and handcuff them. Both CONVICTS look exhausted.

MAGWITCH: Look Sergeant! I've given him up to you. I have stopped him from getting off the marshes.

CONVICT turns to the people of the village.

CONVICT: You are witnesses. This evil, black hearted Negro – He-he-he tried to murder me.

MAGWITCH: Look here! Single handed I got clear of the prison ship; I could have got clear of these marshes – look at my leg – I got rid of the iron. Then I found out – *he* was here. *Him* go free? *Him* profit and make a fool of me again? *He* ruined my life. If it wasn't for *him,* I'd still be a free man.

CONVICT: Officer. He tried to murder me. If you hadn't come when you did, I'd be a dead man.

MAGWITCH: Liar! Look at his face – 'liar' is written all over it. Let him look me in the eye.

The CONVICT looks at the sky and the soldiers but won't look at MAGWITCH.

MAGWITCH: See? See what a villain he is? See those grovelling wandering eyes? That's how he looked when we were tried together in Court. He never looked at me.

CONVICT: You are not much to look at.

MAGWITCH roars with fury and lunges at the CONVICT again. The SOLDIERS have to pull them apart.

SERGEANT: Enough! Light the torches!

One of the soldiers lights some torches and the two convicts quieten down. Another soldier lights a flare/sounds a gun shot twice to signify the convicts have been caught. MAGWITCH turns and looks at JOE and PIP. He stares at PIP for a while, full of emotion. PIP looks terrified.

SERGEANT: We will wait here. The boat will be here soon to take you back to the ship.

The CONVICT slumps to the floor. MAGWITCH keeps his eyes averted from PIP.

MAGWITCH: I wish to say something respecting this escape. It may prevent some persons being under suspicion.

SERGEANT: You can say what you like. It won't make any difference.

MAGWITCH: This is a separate point. A man can't starve. At least I can't. I took some rice and a chicken up at the village over there.

SERGEANT: You mean you stole?

MAGWITCH: From the Cobbler's place.

JOE: My wife said she was missing a couple of hens.

JOE turns to look at MRS GARGERY who nods. For once she seems stunned into silence.

MAGWITCH: So you're the cobbler? Then I'm sorry to say, I cooked and ate your chickens.

JOE: God knows you're welcome to them – so far as they were ever mine. We don't know what you've done, but we wouldn't have you starving to death for it, poor miserable fellow creature. *(JOE does a namasté to MAGWITCH.)* Would we Pip?

PIP shakes his head and MAGWITCH turns his back to them. PIP watches as MAGWITCH's shoulders shake as he sobs quietly.

SOLDIER: Here comes the boat!

The SOLDIERS roughly haul CONVICT up and push MAGWITCH to move. MAGWITCH turns one last time to look at PIP as if he were going to the gallows – and then exits. The SOLDIERS throw the torches into the river to put them out.

SCENE 5

JOE is working on some shoes, hammering and pasting soles on, etc. PIP sits nearby with a young friend BIDDY. He is concentrating hard, writing on a slate and BIDDY is helping him.

BIDDY: Here, try and keep your letters smaller…

PIP: It's hard to keep control…your handwriting's so neat Biddy.

BIDDY: That's because I've had a lot of practice. If you did this every day.

PIP: Every night before I go to bed.

BIDDY: Best to do it in the mornings when your mind's alert.

PIP: That means getting up extra early.

JOE walks over to have a look.

JOE: Pip *beta*! What a scholar you are.

PIP: I'd like to be. How do you spell Gargery, Joe?

JOE: I don't spell it at all.

BIDDY: You can't read or write?

JOE: Very slowly.

BIDDY: Why didn't you go to school Joe?

JOE: My father – he was a drinker. When he was thoroughly drunk, he'd hammer away at my mother. And then he'd hammer away at me. Consequence, my mother and me ran away from my father several times So, it was a bit of a drawback to my learning. But I was good with my hands and I could make a living as a cobbler.

PIP: Is it a real inconvenience having me around?

JOE: When I first got to know your sister, everyone was talking about how she was bringing you up. Very kind of her too. That's what they all said. And so, when I asked for her hand, I told her to bring the poor little child. Kali bless the child, I said. There's room for him at my house.

PIP rushes over and hugs JOE who hugs him back.

JOE: We'll always be the best of friends Pip.

The hug dissolves into tickling and tussling and much hilarity. BIDDY laughs as she watches them both. MRS GARGERY enters, carrying some vegetables from the market.

MRS GARGERY: Well, here's a lovely sight. Me walking all the way back from the market in the hot sun and you lot having fun.

PIP rushes forward and takes the things off MRS GARGERY.

MRS GARGERY: Go on Biddy, run off home now. Your aunt's wondering where you are.

BIDDY: Is she?

MRS GARGERY: Do as you're told.

BIDDY: I'll see you on Saturday morning at school.

PIP: Thanks Biddy!

BIDDY and PIP wave at each other as BIDDY exits.

MRS GARGERY: If this boy isn't grateful today, he never will be.

JOE: Grateful for what?

MRS GARGERY: Miss Havisham wants him.

JOE: The English lady? The one who owns all the land round here?

MRS GARGERY: She doesn't own the land. The Government does you fool.

JOE: But I thought…

MRS GARGERY: Her old father was a trader from the East India company. Now she's an old lady who just lives on her own in that big house.

JOE: What does she want Pip for?

MRS GARGERY: To 'play'.

JOE: Why?

MRS GARGERY: Why not?

JOE: How did she know about Pip?

MRS GARGERY: She asked Uncle Pumblechook to help her find a local boy who would go to her house and play there.

PIP: I don't want to go there… they say there are ghosts in that house.

MRS GARGERY: I've given Uncle my word. You *will* go…or else.

JOE: What is he going to play at?

MRS GARGERY: I don't know.

PIP: *(In tears.)* When do I have to go?

MRS GARGERY: Now.

PIP: No!

MRS GARGERY: What did you just say?

JOE: Those white foreigners…they treat youngsters like Pip very badly. Remember what they did to Ram's boy? Took him in to that big house so far away from home, only nine years old, then they beat him black and blue just because he didn't polish their plates properly.

PIP: Please Joe, don't make me go to Miss Havisham's.

JOE: Sometimes I've heard they take them across the seas, all the way back to their country to serve them in their palaces.

MRS GARGERY: You'll stay at Uncle Pumblechook's tonight and then my uncle has kindly agreed to accompany you, first thing in the morning.
(Turns her attention on PIP.) Right boy, I am going to have to scrub you from head to foot. Can't have you going to Miss Havisham's looking like a village urchin.

MRS GARGERY starts to scrub PIP.

JOE: No! What do we know of this Miss Havisham?

MRS GARGERY: She's a rich old lady, that's all we need to know.

JOE: She wants a servant?…Pip's no servant…

MRS GARGERY: She didn't say anything about needing a servant. You're the one making all these stories up.

JOE: Pip'll have a trade in a few years time…

MRS GARGERY: A trade? As a shoe maker? Hah!

JOE: But Pip's never been away from home.

MRS GARGERY: Well it's time he became a man! He can't hang around here forever, leeching off us.

JOE: At least let me go and speak to this foreign lady first – find out what she wants him to play at.

MRS GARGERY: *You*? Speak to a Memsahib?

MRS GARGERY laughs uproariously at the thought.

JOE: These foreigners are no good. Their ways are strange. They live like Gods… and they don't even pray to the same Gods.

MRS GARGERY: Why do you have to come up with so many objections? This could be the making of the boy!

JOE: What if this Memsahib humiliates him?

MRS GARGERY: Enough! You are a backward, ignorant man – Joe Gargery…This could be the making of Pip or do you want him to grow up to be a poor cobbler like you? You want him to fester in this stinking village for the rest of his life? Working night and day – for what?

JOE looks at PIP guilty.

JOE: I only want the best for Pip.

MRS GARGERY: There's no point of being frightened of progress.

MRS GARGERY takes PIP by the ear and marches him out.

SCENE 6

It is early morning. PUMBLECHOOK leads PIP to MISS HAVISHAM'S estate. As they walk, PUMBLECHOOK coaches PIP.

PUMBLE CHOOK: Boy, be forever grateful to all friends, but especially to them which brought you up by hand.

Now, repeat after me. How do you do?

PIP: How-do-you-do.

PUMBLECHOOK: My name is Pip.

PIP: My name is Pip.

PUMBLECHOOK: It is very nice of you to invite me here for tea.

PIP: Very nice…

PUMBLECHOOK: It *is* very nice.

PIP: It is very nice of you…

PUMBLECHOOK: You will make a total fool of yourself.

They arrive and PUMBLECHOOK raps loudly on the door. A voice from above calls out.

ESTELLA: *(OS.)* What name?

PUMBLECHOOK looks around for where the voice is coming from, slightly confused.

PUMBLECHOOK: How do you do. My name is Pumblechook!

PUMBLE HOOK and PIP wait. The door is opened and a young girl opens the door. She is dressed in English clothes and is very beautiful. She is carrying a large bunch of keys. PUMBLECHOOK looks with interest at ESTELLA who is very striking to look at. PUMBLECHOOK pushes PIP forwards.

PUMBLECHOOK: This is Pip.

ESTELLA: Oh…this is Pip is it? Come in Pip.

PIP steps forward, hesitantly, PUMBLECHOOK steps forward too, but ESTELLA stops him.

ESTELLA: Did you wish to see Miss Havisham?

PUMBLECHOOK: If Miss Havisham wishes to see me.

ESTELLA: Ah! But you see she don't.

ESTELLA is haughty and firm. PUMBLECHOOK looks crestfallen but steps back. Instead he looks at PIP angrily.

PUMBLECHOOK: Boy! Let your behaviour here be a credit to those that brought you up by hand.

ESTELLA shuts the door on PUMBLECHOOK'S face.

PUMBLECHOOK tries to collect his dignity and then exits. ESTELLA turns to PIP.

ESTELLA: Come on Boy!

PIP holds back.

ESTELLA What are you waiting for?

PIP is silent, confused.

ESTELLA grabs PIP by the scruff of his shirt and tugs him. PIP follows ESTELLA through the house. She carries a candle through darkened rooms so that PIP can't make out anything except that it is a big house. Eventually, ESTELLA stops.

ESTELLA: Go in.

PIP: Memsahib.

ESTELLA: Don't be ridiculous boy. I am not going in.

ESTELLA walks away, with the candle, leaving PIP in the dark. He hesitates and then pushes open the door. He walks through into a large room lit by candles but with no natural light. It is a dressing room and sat in the middle on an armchair is an elderly white lady – MISS HAVISHAM. The lady is dressed in faded satins, silks and lace, jewels around her neck and hands and a long yellowy/white veil drapes from her white hair. PIP takes in the surroundings – a trunk overflowing with more silks, a prayer book on the table, etc. PIP notices the cobwebs that hang from the candlesticks and the dried flowers, withered on the dressing table.

MISS HAVISHAM: Who is it?

PIP hesitates. MISS HAVISHAM beckons PIP closer. PIP moves slowly forward.

PIP: How do you do Miss Havisham.

MISS HAVISHAM: What is your name?

PIP: My name is Pip, Memsahib.

MISS HAVISHAM: Pip? Ah, you must be Pumblechook's boy – come to play?

PIP: To play – yes – Memsahib.

MISS HAVISHAM: Come nearer; let me look at you.

PIP does as he is told. He looks up at a clock which has stopped at twenty minutes to nine o'clock and notices that MISS HAVISHAM only has one shoe on. The other sits discarded nearby. It is almost as if the woman has not finished getting dressed.

MISS HAVISHAM: Look at me. You are not afraid of a woman who has never seen the sun since you were born?

PIP shakes his head, afraid.

MISS HAVISHAM touches her left breast with both hands.

MISS HAVISHAM: Do you know what I touch here?

PIP: Yes, Memsahib…

MISS HAVISHAM: What do I touch?

PIP: Your heart.

MISS HAVISHAM: Broken!

PIP steps back a little, afraid by the strange woman.

I am tired. I want diversion and I have done with men and women. Play!

PIP stands stock still.

MISS HAVISHAM: Play! Go on!

PIP remains stock still and silent.

MISS HAVISHAM: Are you rude and obstinate?

PIP: No Memsahib. I can't play…but if you complain about me, I shall get into trouble with my sister, so I would if I could but it's so new and so strange and different and… fine…and sad…here…

MISS HAVISHAM: So new to him, so old to me; so strange to him, so familiar; but so sad to both of us.

Call Estella!

PIP hesitates again.

Call Estella, you can do that can't you?

PIP: *(Calls.)* Memsahib Estella!

ESTELLA'S candle light approaches.

ESTELLA: What is it boy?

PIP: Lady Havisham called you…

ESTELLA pushes past PIP and goes forward into the room. PIP follows her in. MISS HAVISHAM is playing with some sparkly jewels on her dressing table. She beckons ESTELLA towards her. ESTELLA approaches MISS HAVISHAM who holds up the jewels to her neck.

MISS HAVISHAM: Ah my African princess. These will be yours one day, my dear and you will use them well. Let me see you play cards with this boy.

ESTELLA gives PIP a look of utter disdain. As MISS HAVISHAM puts away the jewels.

ESTELLA: With this boy? But he is a common village boy.

MISS HAVISHAM bends closer to ESTELLA and speaks softly to her.

MISS HAVISHAM: Well, you can break his heart.

ESTELLA: *(To PIP.)* Do you know how to play anything, boy?

PIP nods.

MISS HAVISHAM: Play Beggar My Neighbour. Beggar him.

ESTELLA fetches a pack of cards and she and PIP sit down to play cards.

ESTELLA wins at every hand, while PIP looks around the room from time to time. MISS HAVISHAM watch them both. ESTELLA leans forward and inspects PIP's hands. She grimaces.

ESTELLA: This boy has very rough hands! And look at his clothes, such cheap cotton…

PIP looks at his hands helplessly. ESTELLA bends forward and sniffs at PIP. She pulls a disgusted face.

ESTELLA: Euch…the smell!

PIP understands this and looks upset.

ESTELLA: He probably doesn't even use soap. I can smell the village wood fire on all his clothes.

PIP tries to deal the cards but drops them all.

PIP scrabbles around the floor and picks up all the cards.

ESTELLA: He's useless.

PIP: Sorry Memsahib Estella.

ESTELLA: Listen to the way he says 'Memsahib'. He is so common and coarse.

PIP deals again.

ESTELLA: Oh do hurry up boy! Such a clumsy village idiot.

PIP deals on in silence and then drops his cards again. ESTELLA throws up her hands in dismay.

ESTELLA: This is ridiculous. How can I play with such a stupid Indian boy? He probably lives in a stinking mud hut and sleeps on a bed of straw.

ESTELLA walks haughtily away. PIP looks down at his feet.

MISS HAVISHAM beckons PIP over.

MISS HAVISHAM: She says many hard things of you, but you say nothing of her. What do you think of her?

PIP: I don't like to say.

MISS HAVISHAM: Tell me in my ear.

PIP: I think she's very proud.

MISS HAVISHAM: Anything else?

PIP: I think she is very pretty.

MISS HAVISHAM: Anything else?

PIP: I think she is very insulting.

MISS HAVISHAM: Anything else?

PIP: I think I should like to go home.

MISS HAVISHAM: And never see her again, though she is so pretty?

PIP: I'm not sure I shouldn't like to see her again, but I should like to go home, now.

MISS HAVISHAM: When shall I have you here again? Let me think...

PIP: Today is Wednesday.

MISS HAVISHAM waves PIP's words away.

MISS HAVISHAM: I don't care about days of the week, or weeks of the year...come again after six days. You hear?

PIP: Yes Memsahib.

MISS HAVISHAM: Estella, take him down. Let him have something to eat and let him roam and look around while he eats. Go Pip.

PIP follows ESTELLA out with the candle, back through the dark passages. Eventually they come outside again and the bright sunlight temporarily blinds PIP.

ESTELLA disappears for a moment and comes back with a plate of food and a drink. She almost throws the food at PIP. PIP looks shocked but he keeps silent. As ESTELLA exits again, PIP puts down the plate and stares at his hands. Then he examines the texture of his clothes and sniffs his body. Suddenly an overwhelming feeling of shame takes him over. He kicks the wall and pulls his own hair, punishing himself. He sits, shakes and sobs.

ESTELLA watches him from a distance. She looks deeply satisfied by PIP's tears.

Eventually his sobs subside and he eats hungrily.

ESTELLA comes back through with her bunch of keys.

ESTELLA: Why don't you cry some more?

PIP is silent but he stops crying and looks proud.

ESTELLA: You've been crying till you are half blind and you're about to start again now. I hate you stupid natives. You're smelly, uncivilised, uncouth and ugly. I hate you and your oily hair. You're a savage!

ESTELLA laughs contemptuously. PIP remains silent. ESTELLA unlocks the gate and pushes PIP through roughly. Then she locks the gate behind him. PIP runs and exits.

SCENE 7

Outside the GARAGARY hut, PUMBLECHOOK and MRS GARGERY loom over PIP under a night sky and question him.

PUMBLECHOOK: Well boy? How did you get on?

PIP is silent. MRS GARGERY slaps PIP's face.

MRS GARGERY: Answer Uncle Pumblechook boy!

PIP: Pretty well sir.

PUMBLECHOOK: Pretty well is no answer. Tell us boy.

PUMBLECHOOK makes a swipe at PIP. He ducks.

PIP: I mean…pretty well…

MRS GARGERY wallops PIP when PUMBLECHOOK intervenes.

PUMBLECHOOK: No, leave this to me.

PUMBLECHOOK slaps PIP around the face and then boxes his ears.

What does Miss Havisham look like?

PIP looks panicked for a moment and then he thinks of an answer.

PIP: Very tall and dark.

MRS GARGERY: Is that right?

MR PUMBLECHOOK: That is correct. You see? I know how to extract information from youngsters. It just takes a certain skill.

MRS GARGERY: I wish you could have him all the time Uncle. You know how to deal with him.

MRS GARGERY and PUMBLECHOOK drag PIP over to the fire to interrogate him further. PUMBLECHOOK whacks PIP again over the head.

MR PUMBLECHOOK: Now boy, what was she doing when you went in there?

JOE enters. He stands close to PIP, pleased to see the boy.

PIP: Miss Havisham…she was …she was…sitting in a big… black velvet coach.

They all gasp.

PIP: And her niece – I think that's what she was – Estella handed her cake and wine in through the coach window on a gold plate.

MRS GARGERY: Solid gold?

PIP: Yes! And we all had cake and wine on gold plates. And I got up on the coach behind to eat mine.

MR PUMBLECHOOK: Behind the coach? Why?

PIP: Because she told me to.

MRS GARGERY: Was anyone else there?

PIP: Four dogs.

PUMBLECHOOK: Large or small?

PIP: Immense. And they fought for lamb cutlets out of a silver basket.

MRS GARGERY: Where *was* this coach?

PIP: In Miss Havisham's room. But there weren't any horses attached to it.

MRS GARGERY: Can this be possible Uncle? What's the boy talking about?

PUMBLECHOOK: I think he's probably talking about a sedan chair. She's flighty you know – quite flighty enough to pass her days in a sedan chair.

MRS GARGERY: Did you ever see her in it Uncle?

PUMBLECHOOK: How could I? I've never met her! Men aren't allowed in Miss Havisham's house. They say she has some longstanding grudge against us.

JOE: *(Proud.)* But she let our Pip in there.

PUMBLECHOOK: He's not a man! What did you play there?

PIP: We played with flags. Estella waved a blue one, I waved a red one and Miss Havisham waved one sprinkled all over with little gold stars out of the coach window. And then we all waved our swords and hurrahed.

MRS GARGERY: Where did you get the swords from?

PIP: From the cupboard. And I saw pistols in it and jam and pills. And there was no daylight in the room but it was all lighted up with candles.

PUMBLECHOOK: *That* bit I *have* heard. She hasn't seen the light of day for many a long year.

They all sit and stare at PIP who looks awkward.

PUMBLE CHOOK: She'll do something for that boy.

MRS GARGERY: You think so?

PUMBLECHOOK: Definitely. Maybe an apprenticeship in a good trade. Maybe even schooling.

MRS GARGERY: Or some land?

JOE: Or maybe she'll give Pip one of them dogs that fought over the veal cutlets. That would suit us well, wouldn't it Pip *beta*?

MRS GARGERY: If a fool's head can't express better opinions than that and you have any work to do, you had better go and do it.

PIP looks at JOE full of empathy.

PUMBLECHOOK gets up.

PUMBLECHOOK: It's time for my evening prayers. I'll be off now.

MRS GARGERY: I'll walk part of the way with you. I want to go and tell Mina all about the black velvet coach. *(She turns to PIP and gives him a smack around the head.)* What do you say?

PIP: Thank you Uncle Pumblechook.

MRS GARGERY: What for?

PIP: For giving me this opportunity to better myself.

PUMBLECHOOK: Be grateful boy. That's all I ask of you. Be grateful!

PUMBLECHOOK and MRS GARGERY exit together.

JOE stokes the fire and gathers PIP close to him. They sit in silence for a while.

PIP: Joe, can I tell you something?

JOE: Go on.

PIP: It was all lies.

JOE: What was?

PIP: Everything.

JOE sits back and looks at PIP.

JOE: Black velvet coach?

PIP shakes his head.

JOE: Gold plates? Wine?

PIP shakes his head.

JOE: But at least there were dogs, come on Pip. There were dogs weren't there?

PIP shakes his head even more miserably.

JOE: A puppy? Come on!

PIP: No Joe, there was nothing of the kind.

JOE: Pip old chap… Lies… *(He tuts.)* This won't do.

PIP: I'm so unhappy!

JOE: Why? What made you lie like that?

PIP: There was a girl there.

JOE: Estella?

PIP nods.

So at least you told something true.

PIP: She said my hands were coarse and I smelt.
She was so proud and so…beautiful.

JOE: A foreigner?

PIP: Yes… I wish my hands weren't so coarse…or that my
clothes smelled of wood smoke… That's why I lied…I
think.

JOE: A lie is a lie. And it's wrong.

PIP: I know.

JOE: But you're not common, you're uncommonly clever.
Look at all those words you made only yesterday!

PIP: I'm ignorant and backward Joe.

JOE: But you wrote your name beautifully! You've learnt a lot!

PIP: I've learnt nothing. You think too highly of me.

JOE: You got to start somewhere Pip. You're only young. The
Queen on her throne with her crown on her head can't sit
and write acts of Parliament unless she learnt to write when
she was an unpromoted Queen.

I don't like you going out to play with people who think
you're common and smelly.

PIP looks miserable.

JOE: No need to tell your sister, she'll go on the rampage again. But just don't tell any more lies. That way you'll live well and die happy.

Not even a flag with gold stars?

PIP shakes his head.

JOE tries to stifle a smile.

PIP: Are you angry with me Joe?

JOE: No, *beta*. No.

JOE holds PIP close in the firelight.

SCENE 8

PIP is now following ESTELLA through another dark passage, their way lit by a single candle. He has combed his hair and has obviously made a big effort to look smarter. ESTELLA suddenly stops, turns and looks at PIP. He nearly falls over her.

ESTELLA: Well?

PIP: Well Memsahib?

ESTELLA: Am I pretty?

PIP: Yes. I think you are very pretty.

ESTELLA: Am I insulting?

PIP: Not so much as you were that first time.

ESTELLA: Not so much?

PIP: No.

ESTELLA suddenly slaps PIP very hard. PIP smarts.

ESTELLA: Now? You coarse little monster? What do you think of me now?

PIP: I shall not tell you.

ESTELLA: Because you are going to tell upstairs? Is that it?

PIP: No.

ESTELLA: Why don't you cry again, you little wretch?

PIP: Because I'll never cry for you again.

As they make their way through the dark again, with PIP nursing his slapped cheek, an English man (JAGGERS) passes by them.

JAGGERS: Who do we have here?

JAGGERS peers at PIP in the dark.

ESTELLA: Mr Jaggers. An Indian boy.

JAGGERS: Boy of the neighbourhood – eh?

PIP: Yes Sahib.

JAGGERS pulls PIP close to him and takes a good look at him under the candle light.

JAGGERS: I have a pretty large experience of boys, and you're a bad set of fellows. Behave yourself.

PIP: Thank you sir.

JAGGERS exits into the dark.

ESTELLA guides PIP into a room and then exits. It is a different room from the previous one. MISS HAVISHAM is sat in a chair next to a long table. The table is covered with a yellowing, moth-eaten table cloth where dust and cobwebs with plates and silverware are all laid out as if for a feast. In the middle of it is a large, crumbling object, also covered with cobwebs and creepy crawlies.

HAVISHAM: So. The days have worn away have they?

PIP: Yes Memsahib, today is…

MISS HAVISHAM: I don't want to know what day it is.

MISS HAVISHAM looks at PIP's face closely, lost in thought.

You have such melancholy eyes. Have you been crying?

PIP shakes his head.

And yet there is hope behind those sad eyes.

Hope for a better future? A way out of your misery?

PIP: I am sorry if I look miserable…I don't mean to…but life is hard.

MISS HAVISHAM: Yes! Life is hard. So knowing and yet so young.

You and I understand each other Pip.

Come, walk me! Walk me!

MISS HAVISHAM stands up and reaches out for PIP. PIP goes to her and together they start to walk around the room with MISS HAVISHAM leaning on PIP's shoulder. As they walk, MISS HAVISHAM points at the large object on the table.

MISS HAVISHAM: Pip, what do you think that is? Where the cobwebs are?

PIP shakes his head.

MISS HAVISHAM: It's a great cake. A bride-cake. Mine!

They walk some more. PIP looks at the cake, perplexed.

MISS HAVISHAM: Slower!

They slow down.

MISS HAVISHAM: This is my birthday Pip.

PIP: Happy…

MISS HAVISHAM: I don't suffer it to be spoken of.

On this day of the year, long before you were born, this heap of decay was brought here. It and I have worn away together. The mice have gnawed at it and sharper teeth than the teeth of mice have gnawed at me.

MISS HAVISHAM stares at the yellowing, crumbling table.

MISS HAVISHAM: When the ruin is complete and when they lay me dead in my bride's dress on the bride's table, which shall be done and which will be the finished curse upon him – so much the better if it is done on this day!

MISS HAVISHAM stands and stares at the table for quite some time with PIP standing close by. ESTELLA returns and stands there too.

MISS HAVISHAM Pip, I wish you to come every other day from now on. We will walk together. You, at least, do not judge me.

PIP: If that is what you wish Memsahib

MISS HAVISHAM: That is what I wish. Why have you two not started playing cards?

ESTELLA produces a pack of cards. PIP leads MISS HAVISHAM back to her chair and sits with ESTELLA playing.

ESTELLA is disdainful once more to PIP but does not speak. They play for some time with MISS HAVISHAM watching them greedily.

SCENE 9

It is a sunny day and once more, PIP is eating a plate of food outside. He can hear ESTELLA not far off. She is humming a song. He listens – interested – it is a tune he does not recognise. Suddenly he notices a pale young English boy, dressed smartly in a grey suit staring at him. He seems a very cheerful sort.

PALE YOUNG MAN: Hallo! Who let *you* in?

PIP: Memsahib Estella.

PALE YOUNG MAN: And who gave you permission to prowl about?

PIP: Memsahib Estella.

The PALE YOUNG MAN looks PIP up and down.

PALE YOUNG MAN: Come and fight.

The PALE YOUNG MAN lifts his fists in a boxing pose. PIP stares at him for some time and stands up confused.

PALE YOUNG MAN: They say you Bengalis aren't much good at fighting, that you're cowards, always got your noses in books. C'mon…let's see if it's true…

PIP stands warily.

PALE YOUNG MAN: I ought to give you a reason for fighting. Here it is!

The PALE YOUNG MAN slaps his hands against one another, pulls PIP's hair, does a quick boxing jig, slaps his hands again, dips his head and butts PIP in the stomach. PIP lashes out to hit the PALE YOUNG MAN who laughs.

PALE YOUNG MAN: Aha! Would you!

He begins dancing backwards and forwards, skipping and punching the air while PIP looks on helplessly and nurses his sore stomach.

PALE YOUNG MAN: Laws of the game. Regular rules! Come to the ground and go through the preliminaries. Are you satisfied with the ground?

PIP nods.

PALE YOUNG MAN: Do excuse me for a moment young fellow.

The PALE YOUNG MAN exits quickly and returns with a bottle of water and a sponge.

PALE YOUNG MAN: Available for both!

He starts to strip his jacket, shirt and tie. PIP follows suit so that they are both barechested. The PALE YOUNG MAN steps forward, shakes hands with PIP and then squares up to PIP and dances around again, looking very professional. PIP lifts his fists and makes a jab. The PALE YOUNG MAN falls instantly on his back with a bloody nose. He leaps up, sponges his face and starts all over again. They fight and PIP manages to deck the PALE YOUNG MAN several times. By the end of it, the PALE YOUNG MAN has a bloodied nose. He looks cheerful but battered. Eventually he falls to his knees.

PALE YOUNG MAN: That means you have won.

He gathers his clothes to him.

Good afternoon!

The PALE YOUNG MAN does an elaborate namasté and exits. PIP dresses himself hurriedly as ESTELLA approaches with the keys. She smiles at him.

ESTELLA: Come here…you may kiss me if you like.

PIP bends forward and kisses ESTELLA on the cheek.

PIP: What was that tune you were humming earlier on?

ESTELLA: I wasn't humming.

PIP: Yes you were.

ESTELLA: I tell you I was not!

PIP starts to hum the tune, badly.

ESTELLA: That's not how it goes!

ESTELLA hums the tune correctly. It sounds like a lullaby. PIP laughs. ESTELLA stops abruptly, cross. Then she laughs as well.

ESTELLA: You tricked me. Not as stupid as you look are you?

PIP: It's a nice tune but I don't recognise it.

ESTELLA: It's always been in my head. I don't know where I learnt it.

ESTELLA then pushes PIP out of the gate and locks up.

SCENE 10

BIDDY is sitting on the river bank with PIP. He is reading a book she is writing in a journal.

PIP: What are you writing in there?

BIDDY: Just my journal.

PIP: What do you write about?

BIDDY: Oh – things that I've done, my thoughts…a lot of rubbish really. One day I'll read them when I'm old.

She closes her book shut as PIP tries to sneak a peek.

BIDDY: You never told me what it was like at Miss Havisham's house.

PIP looks up from his book.

PIP: Very strange place. And she's even stranger.

BIDDY: Is she horrible to you?

PIP: No. She always treats me right. Even taught me how to dance.

BIDDY: Show me.

PIP looks doubtful.

BIDDY: I've never seen Sahibs dancing. Please show me.

PIP: You'll laugh.

BIDDY: I won't!

PIP: We don't have any music here.

BIDDY: Just do the movements then.

PIP: I can't do it on my own. You'll have to dance with me.

PIP stands up and pulls BIDDY up.

PIP: I put my hand there.

He puts his hand on her waist.

PIP: You put your hand on my shoulder…there…

And we hold hands.

Now, follow my steps.

PIP leads BIDDY around in a waltz.

PIP: 1,2,3…1,2,3…1,2,3…

BIDDY soon gets the hang of it. She clings a bit tighter to PIP, obviously enjoying the physical closeness. They waltz around together laughing, happy – PIP even whirls her around.

BIDDY and PIP stop dancing.

PIP: As usual Biddy, you learn very quickly.

BIDDY: It's a strange sort of dance isn't it?

PIP: It's the holding hands bit that's a little awkward.

BIDDY: I don't understand though, why do you think Miss Havisham wants you there?

PIP: Asked myself that question hundreds of times. A play mate for Estella? Entertainment for her? Maybe she likes the idea of having a native boy around for tea.

BIDDY: They say she's very wealthy.

PIP: And very unhappy.

BIDDY: Do you think she might set you up somewhere?

PIP: That is my sister's hope. Pumblechook dreams that she'll die and leave me her house and he can convert the whole crumbling mansion into a massive Kali temple!

They both fall about laughing.

PIP: Seriously though, she's never given me any money.

BIDDY: And this…Estella…

PIP: Yes.

BIDDY: What is she like?

PIP: The most beautiful girl in the world.

BIDDY looks away, upset. PIP is oblivious.

PIP: Not clever like you. Not even as nice to be with. She's proud and haughty and changeable. One day quite pleasant, the next day she tells me very energetically that she hates me.

BIDDY: She sounds unhappy too.

PIP: How could anyone be happy in that house? There is no daylight in there.

BIDDY: Are you happy Pip?

PIP: I don't know.

BIDDY: How about now, this minute?

PIP: Yes. I'm very comfortable being here with you.

The sun going down, the quietness of the world, talking pleasantly with you.

BIDDY smiles at PIP.

BIDDY: I don't hate you.

PIP smiles at BIDDY. He leans towards BIDDY.

PIP: You will now.

PIP grabs BIDDY's diary and tries to read it.

BIDDY screams and tries to snatch it but PIP is fast. He whisks it out of reach. They tussle and then PIP runs away with the diary. BIDDY chases him.

BIDDY: Give it back! Give it back!

SCENE 11

PIP stands before MISS HAVISHAM and ESTELLA. He is about fifteen years old now. JOE stands by PIP's side. He looks utterly terrified in his best clothes. He looks resolutely down at his feet.

MISS HAVISHAM: Pip. You are growing tall. Have you not noticed Estella?

ESTELLA: Not really.

MISS HAVISHAM: Joe Gargery. You are the husband of the sister of this boy?

JOE says nothing but continues to look awkwardly down at his feet. PIP nudges JOE. JOE steps forward and addresses PIP throughout this scene.

JOE: Well Pip, when I happened to marry your sister, I was single.

MISS HAVISHAM: And you have reared the boy with the intention of taking him for your apprentice, is that so, Mr Gargery?

PIP nudges JOE again, trying to get JOE to address MISS HAVISHAM. JOE is silent. ESTELLA smiles mischievously.

MISS HAVISHAM: Has the boy ever made any objection? Does he like the trade?

JOE: Well Pip, we were ever friends, there was never any objection on your part.

PIP: I suppose I will work with Joe as a cobbler.

MISS HAVISHAM: Is that what you want out of life?

PIP: I am a poor village boy.

MISS HAVISHAM: With very little education.

PIP: I'm afraid so.

MISS HAVISHAM: And what about Estella. Does she not grow prettier and prettier every day?

PIP: *(Shy.)* Yes, she does.

MISS HAVISHAM: And Estella, what do you think of young Pip?

ESTELLA: I hate him.

JOE looks up momentarily confused.

MISS HAVISHAM: Break their hearts my pride and hope! Break their hearts and have no mercy!

MISS HAVISHAM takes out a bag of coins and hands them to PIP.

MISS HAVISHAM: Pip, has earned a premium. Here it is. Give it to your master, Pip. There are five hundred rupees in this bag.

PIP gives the bag to JOE. JOE tries to give the bag back to PIP.

MISS HAVISHAM: I should not keep you here any longer. You are growing Pip and should learn a trade now.

JOE: Pip, this is very liberal on your part…generous and unexpected…received and grateful…

JOE gets tied up in his words and falls silent.

MISS HAVISHAM: You will not receive any more from me.

PIP: Am I to come again Miss Havisham?

MISS HAVISHAM: No, Gargery is your master now. You have been a good boy here and that is your reward. Of course, as an honest boy, you will expect no other and no more.

PIP: No. I never expected anything.

MISS HAVISHAM: As for Estella. She is to travel abroad, to get a better education. She no longer needs a play mate.

PIP steals a look at ESTELLA who does not meet his eye, but she does look sad.

MISS HAVISHAM: Goodbye Pip. Joe Gargery.

PIP: Goodbye Miss Havisham…Miss Estella.

PIP takes his leave and bustles JOE outs.

SCENE 12

We are back outside now down by the river. PIP is reading a book, whilst BIDDY is sat next to him. PIP is older now but wearing work clothes. His face is dirty and his clothes are a little shabby.

PIP: "My heart aches, and a drowsy numbness pains
My sense, as though of hemlock I had drunk,
Or emptied some dull opiate to the drains
One minute past, and Lethe-wards had sunk."

Keats. I love his poetry! I want to be able to read more. The more books I get, the more I want to devour...Shelly, Byron...Shakespeare.

BIDDY: *(Recites.)* "Long sunk in superstition's night,
By Sin and Satan driven,
I saw not, cared not for the light
That leads the blind to Heaven...

But now, at length thy grace, O Lord!
Birds all around me shine;
I drink thy sweet, thy precious word,
I kneel before thy shrine!"

That's an Indian poet's work – Michael Madhusadan Dutta's.

PIP looks amazed.

BIDDY: You should try reading some other Indian writers... like Bankim Chandra Chatterjee's work and...There are many, many new Indians writing now. They write about changing our ideas, about religion, about the loss of our land to foreigners.

PIP: I have heard about them. But I'm not interested in them...

BIDDY: Why not? They say that they are just as clever as the English ones. You're so dismissive.

MRS GARGERY bustles by. She stops momentarily and eyes BIDDY and PIP irritated.

MRS GARGERY: Reading poetry again when there's so much work to be done! Pip, I want you back in five minutes.

PIP: Yes *Didi*.

MRS GARGERY exits.

PIP: Biddy, I want to be a gentleman.

I am not at all happy as I am. I hate my job and my life. I want to lead a very different life from the one I have. It's a most miserable thing to feel ashamed of home.

BIDDY: How can you be ashamed of your home? Your family? Joe...?

PIP looks wracked with guilt.

PIP: I know! I feel so...ungrateful! Just like my sister always said I was. If I could have settled down and been as fond of making shoes as I was when I was little...it would have been much better for me.

PIP: Instead, look at me. Dissatisfied and uncomfortable – because Estella told me long ago I was a coarse and common Indian boy.

BIDDY: That was neither a very true nor a very polite thing of her to say.

PIP: She's even more beautiful than anybody ever was, and I admire her dreadfully; and I want to be a gentleman on her account.

BIDDY: Do you want to be a gentleman to spite her, or to gain her over?

PIP: I don't know.

BIDDY: Because if it's to spite her it might be better to care nothing for her words and if it's to gain her over – she was not worth gaining in the first place.

PIP: You may be right but I can't stop loving her.
And I feel so coarse and – black and dirty. I dread her seeing me hunched over leather, making shoes. She would laugh at me and I all I want is to be her equal. I am the lowest of the low!

PIP rolls over onto the grass and cries.

BIDDY comforts him.

PIP: I wish you could fix me.

BIDDY: I wish I could.

PIP: I don't want to be a cobbler. I want to be someone.

BIDDY: You should have got a proper education, gone to school. You're a bright young man and you're frustrated. It's nothing to do with Estella. You're focussed on her because she was…

PIP: Completely unattainable. Is that the human way – to want what you can't have? *You* should have gone to a proper school, you're cleverer than I am and yet you always seem happy.

BIDDY looks away. She doesn't know what to say.

PIP: What is it Biddy?

BIDDY shakes her head and gets up and brushes herself down.

PIP: Are you angry with me?

BIDDY shakes her head again. She turns her face away from PIP.

PIP: Please tell me. You're my best friend in the world. The only person I can talk to about my feelings.

BIDDY: I have to get back. I promised my aunt I would read to her tonight.

BIDDY rushes off. PIP watches her go, confused.

SCENE 13

It is dusk. MRS GARGERY is busy sweeping the yard when she hears a commotion near the hut – clattering pans being overturned, hens squawking, etc. She picks up 'tickler' and approaches the hut.

MRS GARGERY: Who's there?

Come out where I can see you.

This is private property. Pip? Pip? Is that you?

An unknown man in the darkness rushes out. MRS GARGERY attacks him with 'tickler' and starts to hit him viciously.

MRS GARGERY: How dare you! Thief! People like you, scum of the earth, stealing from honest, hard working folk. They should string you up!

The man grabs 'tickler' off MRS GARGERY and beats her over the head with it. MRS GARGERY for once in her life is overpowered. The man beats her up and MRS GARGERY collapses. The man then grabs all the hens and a bag of rice and runs. PIP runs in at the end shouting. He sees his sister lying on the floor and goes to her. There is blood all over her face.

PIP: *Didi! Didi!*

SCENE 14

PIP and JOE are sat on the ground working on making shoes, outside their little hut. PIP is 18 years old. They hear the sound of horse hooves and a carriage nearby as it draws up. A man calls out.

JAGGERS: *(OS.)* Is this the abode of Mr Joe Gargery?

JOE looks up at PIP in amazement.

JOE: An English man? Here?

PIP: *(Calls out.)* Yes!

JAGGERS: *(OS.)* You have an apprentice commonly known as Pip? Is he here?

JOE looks anxious.

JOE: Shall I hide you? What does an English man want with you? Maybe it's the law?

PIP: I have done nothing wrong.

(Calls out.) I am here!

JAGGERS enters. He is the same English man PIP met briefly at MISS HAVISHAM's. He is suited and looking hot from his travels.

JAGGERS: Ah…are you Joe Gargery and…Pip?

PIP: We are.

JAGGERS: I wish to have a private conference with you two. It will take a little time.

JAGGERS looks down at the ground and looks anxious because he can't sit down.

PIP gets up and brings forward a stool. JAGGERS sits down on it. JOE brings the man a glass of water which JAGGERS sniffs before he sips it.

JAGGERS: My name is Jaggers and I am a lawyer from Calcutta. I am pretty well known.

JAGGERS hands his card over to JOE who takes it but doesn't look at it.

JAGGERS: I have unusual business to transact with you and I commence by explaining that it is not of my originating. If my advice had been asked, I should not have been here. It was not asked and you see me here. What I have to do as the confidential agent of another, I do. No less, no more.

JAGGERS: Now Joseph Gargery, I am the bearer of an offer to relieve you of this young fellow your apprentice. You would not object to this, at his request and for his good? You would not want anything for so doing?

JOE: Kali forbid that I should want anything for standing in Pip's way.

JAGGERS: Kali forbidding is pious, but not to the purpose. The question is, would you want anything?

JOE: The answer is 'no'.

JAGGERS: Remember what you have said and don't try and change your mind.

JAGGERS: The communication I have to make is that Mr Pip has great expectations.

PIP and JOE look surprised.

JAGGERS: I am instructed to communicate to him that he will come into a handsome property. Further, that is the desire of the present possessor of that property that he be immediately removed from his present sphere of life and from this place and be brought up as a gentleman – in a word, as a young fellow of great expectations.

Now Mr Pip. You are to understand, first, that this is the request of the person from whom I take my instructions, that you always bear the name of Pip. You have any objection to that?

PIP: N…no…no objection.

JAGGERS: I should think not! Now you are to understand, secondly, Mr Pip, that the name of the person who is your liberal benefactor remains a profound secret until the person chooses to reveal it. I am empowered to mention that it is the intention of the person to reveal it at first hand by word of mouth to yourself. When or where that intention may be carried out, I cannot say; no one can say. It may be years hence. Now you are distinctly to understand that you are most positively prohibited from making any inquiry on this head, or any allusion or reference, however distant, to any individual whomsoever as *the* individual, in all the communications you have with me. If you have a suspicion in your own breast, keep in there. Do you have any objection to this stipulation?

PIP: N…no…no objection.

BIDDY enters leading MRS GARGERY IN by the hand who leans on her. MRS GARGERY looks disabled and has to be helped into a chair. BIDDY listens to the conversation with interest.

JAGGERS: I should think not! Now Mr Pip, I have done with stipulations. We come next to mere details of arrangement. There is already lodged in my hands a sum of money amply sufficient for your suitable education and maintenance. You will please consider me your guardian. You will be educated to be an English gentleman. There is a certain tutor of whom I have some knowledge who I think might suit the purpose. The gentleman I speak of is Mr Matthew Pocket.

There is quite a crowd of villagers listening in now.

PIP: I am much obliged for the recommendation.

JAGGERS: I do not recommend him, I am simply saying he will suit the purpose.

PIP: I am much obliged for the mention of Mr Pocket.

JAGGERS: That's more like it.

First, you should have some new clothes to come to Calcutta in and they should not be working clothes. Say this day week. You'll want some money, shall I leave you fifty rupees?

JAGGERS hands over a purse of money. JOE gasps.

JAGGERS: Well Joseph Gargery? You look dumb founded.

JOE: It's all so sudden.

JAGGERS: Your charge is my charge from now on. I will be unburdening you.

JOE: I have never seen my Pip as a burden…

JAGGERS: Nevertheless…

JOE: And you are assuming that he will want to go with you to the city. He may not want to go. He has been here with us all his life, he has a trade, people that care for him...

JOE looks across at BIDDY.

JOE: ...who love him. Where will he get that in the City?

JAGGERS softens a little.

JAGGERS: All birds must fly the nest and what I offer young Master Pip is a glittering future.

JOE: *(Looks at PIP.)* What do you say?

PIP looks from JAGGERS to JOE.

PIP: I...I...

JOE: Don't let this gentleman bully you into anything.

It's your life. Your decision.

PIP: I want to go Joe.

JOE tries to hide his upset. He pulls PIP aside.

JOE: But you don't know anyone in the city. Not a soul. Won't you be lonely? Who will look after you when you fall ill? And these foreigners Pip...can they be trusted? How do we know this man isn't just trying to steal you away?

PIP: Why would he single me out though Joe? I'm not very special.

JOE: You *are* special. What if they mistreat you or force you into some kind of servitude?

PIP: It's a chance worth taking.

JOE: You could lose your liberty, your soul, your...they might make you eat the flesh of cows!

PIP: I'll get an education.

JOE: *(Looks at JAGGERS.)* Can't he do his learning here?

JAGGERS looks rather sniffily around the village and at the rag tag bunch of villagers.

JAGGERS: I think not. But what if it was my instructions to make you a present, as compensation?

JOE: As compensation for what?

JAGGERS: For the loss of Mr Pip's services.

JOE: If you think money can make compensation to me for the loss of the little child that came into my house all those years ago...ever the best of friends...

JAGGERS: I warn you Joe Gargery, this is your last chance.

JOE squares up to JAGGERS who cowers.

JOE: You come in to my house and try and badger and bully me...

PIP draws JOE away immediately. JAGGERS gets up and backs away.

JOE: Is this what you want Pip? To be...one of them?

JOE eyes JAGGERS with distaste.

PIP looks torn.

PIP: I want a chance in life.

JOE: To go away from us? From this village?

PIP: Yes.

JOE: Then you must go. If that's where your heart lies, you must follow your heart.

JAGGERS: Well Mr Pip, I think the sooner you leave this place, as you are to be a gentleman, the better. Let it stand for this day week. I will send you instructions on how to get there.

JAGGERS tips his hat and then suddenly notices the villagers who have all gathered to hear PIP's news. He looks a little afraid and hurriedly exits. We hear the horse drawn carriage gallop off and the villagers all cheer and dance around PIP. Indian sweetmeats are brought, garlands of flowers are laid at PIP's feet and there are general celebrations.

Only JOE and BIDDY watch on sadly.

SCENE 15

PIP stands in front of a mirror. He is dressing himself in an English suit and shirt and is trying his cravat. BIDDY enters.

PIP: You know, I shall never forget you.

BIDDY: You'll come back won't you? From time to time?

PIP: Of course. But you will help Joe on a little won't you?

BIDDY: Help him on?

PIP: It's just that Joe is such a dear man – in fact I think he's the best man that ever lived – but he's rather backward in some things. You know, in his learnings and his manners.

BIDDY: Won't his manners do then?

PIP: They do very well *here* in the village.

BIDDY is silent.

But if I were to remove Joe into a higher sphere, as I shall hope to remove him when I fully come into my property, then they would hardly do him justice.

BIDDY: And don't you think he knows that?

PIP: What do you mean?

BIDDY: Have you never considered that he may be proud?

PIP: Proud?

BIDDY: Oh! There are many different kinds of pride.

Pride is not only of one kind...

BIDDY looks pointedly at PIP.

PIP: What are you stopping for?

BIDDY: Not all of one kind. He may be too proud to let anyone take him out of a place that he is competent to fill and fills well with respect. To tell you the truth, I think he is: though it sounds bold in me to say so, for you must know him far better than I do.

PIP: I did not expect to see this in you. You are envious and grudging. You are unhappy on account of my rise to fortune.

BIDDY: If you have the heart to think that – say so. Say so over and over again.

PIP: It's a bad side of human nature. I did intend to ask you to use any little opportunities you might have after I was gone, for improving dear Joe. But after this, I ask you nothing.

BIDDY: I will always help Joe, whether you scold me or approve of me. But a true gentleman should not be unjust either.

BIDDY turns to go. PIP looks upset.

PIP: You are unjust.

BIDDY: I wish you the best Pip. I always want good fortune for you. This is a wonderful opportunity. Maybe you can be the equal of Estella now. But don't presume that Joe is any less of a man because he can't follow you into English society.

PIP: You don't want me to better myself?

BIDDY: Money does not make you better. It gives you opportunities.

PIP: I want to be someone.

BIDDY: You are someone. You are my Pip. My friend. Never forget where you came from.

Be proud of who you are.

BIDDY stands for a moment and takes one last look at PIP.

BIDDY: Whatever you think of me and Joe, you will always be loved.

BIDDY exits. PIP is irritated.

SCENE 16

PIP now in his new western suit, clutching his hat, stands before MISS HAVISHAM. The crumbling, cobwebbed cake and the yellowy candle lit rooms with the clocks stopped at twenty to nine are all as they were before. Only MISS HAVISHAM seems changed in that she is older and more shrunken into herself.

She peers at PIP.

PIP: I start for Calcutta, Miss Havisham tomorrow.

MISS HAVISHAM: This is a handsome figure Pip.

PIP: I have come into such good fortune since I last saw you Miss Havisham. And I am so grateful for it!

MISS HAVISHAM: Good. Good. I have seen Mr Jaggers. I have heard about it Pip. So you go tomorrow?

PIP: Yes, Miss Havisham.

MISS HAVISHAM: And you are adopted by a rich person?

PIP: Yes Miss Havisham.

MISS HAVISHAM: Not named?

PIP shakes his head.

MISS HAVISHAM: And Mr Jaggers is made your guardian?

PIP: Yes Miss Havisham.

MISS HAVISHAM: And already, you have stopped calling me 'Memsahib'.

PIP: I'm s-s-sorry…perhaps I…

MISS HAVISHAM waves away PIP'S apologies.

MISS HAVISHAM: And you almost look like an English gentleman already.

PIP: I want to make something of my life.

MISS HAVISHAM: Well! You have a promising career before you. Perhaps in time, you could even travel to London, study at the Bar, make your fortune. Be good Pip. Deserve it and abide by Mr Jaggers instructions. You will always keep the name of Pip, you know.

PIP: Yes Miss Havisham.

How is…how is…?

MISS HAVISHAM: Estella?

PIP: Yes!

MISS HAVISHAM: I have sent her away to London to become a Lady. She is more beautiful than ever and admired by all who see her. They call her the 'Black beauty of Calcutta'.

PIP: Will you please send her my…fondest regards.

MISS HAVISHAM: I will. Do you still love her Pip?

PIP: I do.

MISS HAVISHAM draws PIP closer to her.

MISS HAVISHAM: Love her! Love her! Love her!

If she favours you, love her! If she wounds you, love her! If she tears your heart to pieces – and as it gets older and stronger, it will tear deeper – love her, love her, love her!

PIP stands back and looks shocked by MISS HAVISHAM's passion.

MISS HAVISHAM: I adopted her to be loved. I bred her and educated her to be loved. I developed her into what she is, that she might be loved. Love her!

I'll tell you what real love is. It is blind devotion, unquestioning self humiliation, utter submission, trust and belief against yourself and against the whole world, giving up your whole heart and soul to the smiter – as I did!

MISS HAVISHAM cries out loud, stands in her chair and then collapses. PIP has to catch her and help her back into her chair.

MISS HAVISHAM: Goodbye Pip.

PIP bends down and touches MISS HAVISHAM's feet in pranam.

ACT II

CALCUTTA

SCENE 1

PIP arrives in Calcutta. Some kind of stage craft to show the crowds and the life of the place. Sound of mosque's Muezzin's call as well as Hindu chanting. PIP wanders around, looking at the sights and sounds. He is amazed and frightened at the same time. He is carrying a small Indian bag with all his worldly possessions.

An Indian man WEMICK catches hold of PIP.

WEMICK: Name's Wemick.

    PIP looks at WEMICK unsure.

WEMICK: I'm Mr Jaggers' clerk.

    PIP looks relieved.

WEMICK: He's busy at the moment but I am to take you to his rooms.

    WEMICK looks down at PIP'S bag confused.

The rest of your luggage?

PIP: This is it.

    WEMICK leads the way and they walk. We see the life of the streets of Calcutta around them. PIP is trying to take this all in and looking about him at the same time.

WEMICK: You've never been to Calcutta before?

PIP: No.

WEMICK: *I* was new here once. Funny to think of it now.

PIP: Which part are you from?

WEMICK: Bolpur. Where the earth is red between your toes.

PIP: Do you go back there at all?

WEMICK: I tried, a few times but…the country life doesn't suit me so well anymore. Quiet. Too quiet and too many mosquitoes, not that there aren't mosquitoes here. Different kind.

PIP: You are well acquainted with Calcutta now?

WEMICK: Yes. I know the moves of it.

PIP: Is it a very wicked place?

WEMICK: You may get cheated, robbed and murdered in Calcutta but there are plenty of people anywhere who'll do that for you.

PIP: Do you have any advice to offer me?

WEMICK: Me? Give *you* advice Mr Pip?

PIP: I am completely new to this life.

WEMICK: Just remember, the white Sahib generally likes to keep to his own. He does not believe we are equal and so however much of a brown Sahib you become, he will never let you enter his inner chambers, if you see what I mean.

PIP: Tell me, what manner of man is Mr Jaggers?

Why is an English man practicing law here?

WEMICK: Someone needs to protect the English out here. Not that he only represents Englishmen.

PIP: He represents Indians too?

WEMICK: If the case seems fair and…Mr Jaggers has no prejudices when it comes to the colour of his clients' money.

PIP: I hardly know what to make of his manner.

WEMICK: Tell him that and he'll take it as a compliment. Always seems to me as if he had set a man trap and was watching it. Suddenly-snap-you're caught!

PIP: I suppose he's very skilfull?

WEMICK: He's certainly well known round here. There's no other Mr Jaggers and no one better to have on your side.

PIP finds his pace slowing to a halt as he sees a small crowd of people gathering around a speaker standing on a soap box.

WEMICK humours PIP and stops with him, although he constantly looks at his pocket watch.

INDIAN MAN: Brothers and sisters – listen to the poetry of a scholar from the Hindu college. An Indian scholar who is steeped in classical texts of Latin, Sanskrit, Persian and Arabic. Listen and learn!

"Long sunk in superstition's night,
By Sin and Satan driven,
I saw not, cared not for the light
That leads the blind to Heaven…
But now, at length thy grace, O Lord!
Birds all around me shine;
I drink thy sweet, thy precious word,
I kneel before thy shrine!"

People around the man stand to appreciate the poem. PIP is drawn to the Indian man.

INDIAN MAN: As long as the Bengali race and Bengali literature exists, the sweet lyre of Madhusadan will never cease playing.

Read my brothers and sisters! Be proud of who you are and take from the Foreigners as they have taken from us! There is a revolution in thoughts and ideas, in religion and life going on here in Calcutta, right under our noses! From the stories of gods and goddesses, kings and queens, princes and princesses we must have faith in our language and our ancestral heritage. Don't just blindly follow the learnings of the west. We have learning too! We have a history that shows that we have expelled invaders before now. Do it through words, through the pen to begin with, be brave!

WEMICK pulls PIP along.

WEMICK: Bengalis, we do like the sound of our own voice.

This way Mr Pip.

They arrive at JAGGERS' office. There are a couple of people waiting for JAGGERS. MAN steps forward and tries to way lay JAGGERS.

JAGGERS: I don't know this man!

MAN: I am Bentley Drummle's brother…

JAGGERS: And?

MAN: I've come to beg you to help him out of his terrible predicament. All he did was…

JAGGERS: …to beat a native woman within an inch of her life. Just because he is English he cannot presume to be able to buy my services.

MAN: But you are the best man for him sir and he could end up languishing in a foreign jail!

JAGGERS: And whose fault is that? I am not interested in Bentley Drummle. He is a scoundrel.

JAGGERS sweeps by, stopping for a moment to look at PIP.

JAGGERS: Mr Pip.

PIP stands slightly confused. WEMICK pushes PIP forward and they both follow JAGGERS to his rooms.

We follow the three men into JAGGERS' office.

JAGGERS is standing in his office. He is eating a sandwich ("he seemed to bully his very sandwich as he ate it") and looking at PIP.

JAGGERS: So Mr Pip, you made it out of your village. Congratulations.

PIP: Thank you sir.

JAGGERS: Wemick, you have given Mr Pip his instructions?

WEMICK turns to PIP.

WEMICK: You're to go to College Street to young Mr Pocket's rooms, where a bed has been sent for your accommodation. You are to remain with young Mr Pocket; on Monday you are to go with him to his father's house on a visit. Your allowance is 150 rupees a month.

MR WEMICK surreptitiously draws out a brown envelope and slips it to PIP.

PIP: That's very kind…

MR JAGGERS: We are not in the habit of being kind Mr Pip, simply following the instructions of my client.

MR WEMICK produces some cards which he also hands over.

WEMICK: And here are some cards of tradesmen with whom you are to deal for clothes and such other things as you could have reason to want.

PIP: Yes.

JAGGERS: You will find your credit good Mr Pip but I shall by this means be able to check your bills and to pull you up if I find you…overspending.

Do you read English?

PIP: A little.

JAGGERS: I have arranged for you to be tutored as you know, by Mr Matthew Pocket… you are not designed for any particular profession but you should be well enough educated to hold your own with prosperous Indian men.

PIP: Erm…yes…

JAGGERS: Do you have any profession you would like to pursue?

PIP: Not really thought about it sir….apart from to be educated.

JAGGERS: With your financial backing young man, you do not need a profession. But you *do* need learning and we need young Indians like you.

It is impossible for us with our limited means, to attempt to educate the body of Indians. So we must do our best to form a class who may be interpreters between us and the millions whom we govern.

PIP: By we, I'm assuming you mean…

JAGGERS: The English of course!
We need young men like you – Indian in blood and colour but English in taste, opinions, in morals and intellect.

PIP: I am keen to learn.

JAGGERS: Good. I am sure Mr Matthew Pocket will do his utmost to educate you into the ways of an English gentleman. That is what my client has expressly related to me.

PIP: I am strong in my belief I will be able to make my benefactor proud of me.

An English maid servant enters with a tray of tea.

JAGGERS: Ah Molly…

MOLLY places the tray down silently.

JAGGERS: Now let me show you something Mr Pip. Molly! Show the young man your wrists.

MOLLY is reluctant.

JAGGERS: Come now Molly.

JAGGERS entraps MOLLY'S hands on the table.

MOLLY: Master – please…

JAGGERS: Let Mr Pip see your wrists.

MOLLY turns both her wrists over to show PIP who stares bemused.

JAGGERS: There's power here. Very few men have the power of wrist that this woman has. It's remarkable what mere force of grip there is in these hands. I have had occasion to notice many hands; but I never saw stronger in that respect, man or woman's, than these.

MOLLY: Do you need me for anything else sir?

JAGGERS: No thank you. That'll do Molly. You have been admired and now you can go.

MOLLY nods and leaves. PIP hears a drum roll from outside the window of JAGGERS' office. There's a sound of a crowd groaning and a woman starts to wail loudly. PIP looks alarmed and leaps up as if to go to the window to take a look.

JAGGERS: Ah now Mr Pip. I wouldn't take a peek if I were you, not unless you have a strong constitution. Gallows my young man. Twenty men and three women hanged just now.

PIP: Hanged?

JAGGERS: Since the English Crown have taken over the governance of India, the laws against sedition and treason are much stricter.

PIP: Who were those people?

JAGGERS: You'll be pleased to know that not one of them was my client. However, they were all connected with insurgencies against the government and Crown.

WEMICK: I don't suppose Mr Pip ever had occasion to see such examples of British Justice in his village.

PIP moves away from the window.

JAGGERS: Indeed.

When you have settled in Mr Pip, you must come to supper. I will send one of the Clerks up to walk you to your lodgings. Come Wemick.

JAGGERS sweeps out of the office.

WEMICK: As I keep the cash, we shall likely meet pretty often. Good day.

WEMICK does a namasté whilst PIP puts out his hand to shake hands.

WEMICK: You're in the habit of shaking hands?

PIP looks a little confused.

PIP: Is that not what gentlemen do in Calcutta?

WEMICK: I have got so out of the habit recently! Very glad, I'm sure to make your acquaintance. Good day!

WEMICK shakes hands and exits. PIP stands in JAGGERS' office looking completely lost.

SCENE 2

PIP stands in some rooms waiting for HERBERT POCKET. He looks bored and keeps looking at his pocket watch. Eventually, a young English man of PIP's age, dressed as a gentleman explodes out of breath through the door. He is weighed down with bags of fruit.

HERBERT POCKET: Mr Pip?

PIP: Mr Pocket?

HERBERT POCKET: Dear me! I am extremely sorry to keep you waiting. I went to the market to get some fruit for your arrival…

HERBERT is struggling with the door.

HERBERT POCKET: Dear me, this door sticks!

PIP: Here, let me help you…

PIP takes the bags off HERBERT who continues to struggle with the door and then suddenly it closes and HERBERT falls back on top of PIP. They both stagger back, fruit tumbling and laugh.

As they both get busy picking up the fruit and bumping heads, they continue to laugh.

HERBERT POCKET: It's rather bare here, but I hope you will be able to make out tolerably well. My father thought you would get on more agreeably with me than him. As to our lodging, it's not by any means splendid, because I have my own bread to earn and my father hasn't anything to give me and I shouldn't be willing to take it, if he had. But dear me, I beg your pardon, you're holding the fruit all this time.

HERBERT POCKET takes the bags off PIP.

PIP: Are you sure…I mean…for me to stay here…it's very kind but is it…proper?

HERBERT POCKET: I'm sorry, I don't…

PIP: I'm Indian. You're…

HERBERT POCKET: Oh! Poppycock! I assure you, we don't stand with any of that nonsense. My father taught me at all times to mix freely with the natives.

HERBERT POCKET looks closely at PIP.

HERBERT POCKET: Lord bless me! I've finally realised why you look so familiar – you're the prowling boy!

PIP: And you are the pale young gentleman!

They both stare at each other amazed.

HERBERT POCKET: What a coincidence. The idea of it being *you!*

They both laugh excitedly again and shake hands heartily.

HERBERT POCKET: Well, well, well…do forgive me if I knocked you about a bit back then. I hope I didn't hurt you too badly?

PIP looks momentarily confused.

PIP: No, not at all.

HERBERT POCKET shows PIP to a chair. He sits down. HERBERT starts fussily arranging the fruit in a bowl. Mangoes, a pineapple, guavas' etc.

HERBERT POCKET: You hadn't come into your good fortune then had you?

PIP: No.

HERBERT POCKET: *I* was rather on the look out for good fortune myself at the time.

PIP: Were you?

HERBERT POCKET: Yes. Miss Havisham sent for me to see if she could take a fancy to me. But she couldn't and she didn't.

PIP: Can't imagine why.

HERBERT POCKET: She obviously had very bad taste.

They both laugh.

HERBERT POCKET: Estella hated me…she's so hard and haughty and capricious and she's been brought up by Miss Havisham to wreak revenge on all the male sex.

PIP: How is she related to Miss Havisham?

HERBERT POCKET: She's adopted.

PIP: But why would she wreak revenge on men?

HERBERT POCKET: Lord Mr Pip. Don't you know the story?

It's quite a long one. Are you hungry?

PIP: Starving.

HERBERT POCKET: Then why don't we save our story 'til lunch?

PIP: Alright then.

How is Estella related to Miss Havisham?

HERBERT: There has always been an Estella since I have heard of a Miss Havisham.

I know no more apart from what I have said – she has been brought up to suit Miss Havisham's strange purposes.

PIP: So she is an orphan.

HERBERT: Nobody knows for certain. My uncle believes she is of mixed blood... a Mulatto... or Arab...but my father thinks she is the product of an illicit relationship between an Indian Prince and an African woman.

PIP is amazed.

PIP: African?!

HERBERT: It's not unheard of.

She's been brought up as a sort of blue blooded black princess. An African English rose – to the extent that she probably believes it herself.

PIP looks flummoxed.

PIP: But the English will never accept her.

HERBERT: My good man. Surely you must know this about us English. If a dark skin person has the good manners, the grace of landed aristocracy and most importantly, the money, Queen Victoria will take them to her bosom.

Mr Jaggers is your guardian, I understand?

PIP: Yes.

HERBERT POCKET: He was very obliging as to suggest my
father for your tutor. Of course he knew about my father
from his connection with Miss Havisham. My father is her
cousin; not that that means anything. He can't stand her
and never goes to visit her.

Still I want to hear all of your history first.

PIP: It's not very interesting but I'll tell you whatever you
want to hear. In the meantime, I don't really have…I'm a
village boy…not sure how to behave sometimes in genteel
company…manners…that sort of thing.

HERBERT POCKET: You seem perfectly civilised to me!

PIP: I'd be grateful if you could correct me if you see me going
wrong at any moment.

HERBERT POCKET: With pleasure though I don't think you'll
need many hints. And please call me Herbert.

PIP: And you must call me Pip.

They shake hands and laugh.

SCENE 3

*HERBERT and PIP are sat at a table in a coffee shop in Calcutta. They
are being served by an Indian waiter.*

*The Muslim waiter places a knife and fork before them both. PIP looks
a little worried when he sees the cutlery.*

HERBERT: You're a man of means now – so you can eat
whatever you want.

PIP: What line of work are you in Herbert?

*The waiter opens the napkins with a flourish and places them on the
men's laps. PIP looks at the napkin on his lap with some concern.*

HERBERT: I am a capitalist – an insurer of ships.

PIP: And there's money in that?

HERBERT: Plenty. I'll take you down to the docks tomorrow and you will see how many ships pass through Calcutta to China, down to the Cape and others headed for the Australian colonies and of course even the prison ships headed for the Andaman islands. They all carry silks, drugs, spices, dyes, precious woods, teas and indeed human cargo to such far flung places. And they all need to be insured.

PIP: And the profits are large?

HERBERT: Tremendous. I think I shall trade also to the West Indies for sugar, tobacco and rum. And to Ceylon, especially for elephants tusks.

PIP: Do you own many ships?

HERBERT: Oh, not at all…not yet anyway.

The waiter enters carrying a tray of mixed kebabs which he starts to serve.

HERBERT starts cutting up his food and eating. PIP picks up a kebab with his fingers. HERBERT watches for a moment and then ostentatiously lifts his cutlery. PIP stops mid-mouthful. He quickly wipes his hands on his napkin and lifts his knife and fork. He mimics HERBERT.

HERBERT: I'm biding my time at Writers building to earn my daily bread. But one day dear Pip, I will make my fortune just like you!

HERBERT: So, you want to hear about Miss Havsiham?

PIP: I'm extremely curious to hear the tale.

PIP puts the kebab in his mouth and chews slowly.

HERBERT: Let me introduce the topic Pip, by mentioning that in Calcutta it is not the custom to put the knife in the mouth – for fear of accidents – and that while the fork is reserved for that use, it is not put further in than is necessary.

PIP: Oh. Sorry.

HERBERT: It is scarcely worth mentioning, only it is well to do as others would.

PIP: Thank you.

HERBERT: Now, concerning Miss Havisham...

She was an only child. Her mother died when she was a baby and her father denied her nothing.

As the two men talk, we see a younger version of MISS HAVISHAM sitting at her dressing table powdering her nose. A maid stands close by pinning her hair.

HERBERT: He used to be an agent for the East India Company and he was very rich and very proud and so was his daughter. She had a half brother. Her father privately married again – his cook.

PIP: His cook??

HERBERT: By all accounts, a very beautiful Indian woman. Yes! It was a bit of a scandal at the time, although not that unusual. Anyway, the second wife also died and the half breed son became part of the family. As the son grew he turned out to be a bit of a philanderer. Riotous, extravagant, undutiful – altogether bad. Eventually his father disinherited him but then must have softened on his death bed. He left some money to his son, but left his daughter, Miss Havisham much better off.

PIP drains his glass of laissi.

HERBERT: Take another glass of *laissi* and excuse my mentioning that society as a body does not expect one to be strictly conscientious in emptying one's glass as to turn it bottom upwards with the rim on one's nose.

PIP laughs and puts down his glass.

PIP: I'm sorry…Thank you.

HERBERT: Not at all.

The young MISS HAVISHAM's Maid is now bedecking MISS HAVISHAM in glittering jewels. PIP is trying to stuff his napkin into his glass.

HERBERT: Miss Havisham was now an heiress and you may suppose was looked after as a great match. Her half brother squandered all his money and she and he argued constantly. It is suspected that he cherished a deep and mortal grudge against her as having influenced her father's anger. Now I will come to the cruel part of the story breaking off, my dear Pip, to remark that a dinner napkin will not go into a tumbler.

PIP: My apologies…thank you.

PIP carefully puts his tumbler down. The waiter comes back and haughtily places another napkin on PIP's lap and a fresh glass of laissi.

HERBERT: Not at all. I'm sure.

A dashing, overly dressy young English man comes to MISS HAVISHAM's dressing table and takes her hand. He leads her away and they dance together. The young MISS HAVISHAM looks absolutely smitten.

HERBERT: There appeared on the scene a certain man who made love to Miss Havisham. I never met him because this all happened over twenty five years ago – before you and I were born Pip. But I have heard my father talk about him. He was a showy man and not a gentleman. My father says that no varnish can hide the grain of wood; and the more varnish you put on, the more the grain will express itself.

The young MISS HAVISHAM and the dashing young man sit closely, holding hands, whispering and laughing together.

HERBERT: She fell passionately in love. He practised on her affection and by various schemes, managed to get vast quantities of money from her. She was too haughty and too much in love to be advised by anyone. Her relations were poor and scheming with the exception of my father. He warned her that she was doing too much for this man and was heading towards disaster. She angrily ordered my father out of her house, in this man's presence, and my father has never seen her since.

The dashing young man goes down on bended knee to MISS HAVISHAM, obviously proposing. She looks delighted. MISS HAVISHAM goes back to her dressing table and starts getting dressed for her wedding. The maid brings in her long white wedding dress, her veil, puts flowers in her hair and brings out her wedding slippers.

HERBERT: Anyway, this man proposed to Miss Havisham and she accepted. The wedding day was fixed. The guests invited.

A large table is brought in, silverware is placed, servants run around as the large wedding cake is placed on the table. The young MISS HAVISHAM continues to dress.

HERBERT: The honeymoon tour was planned, the house was bedecked fit for a royal wedding.

As MISS HAVISHAM places one shoe on, a messenger arrives with a letter. She eagerly rips it open, recognising her lover's handwriting. As she reads, she recoils in horror.

HERBERT: The day came, but not the groom. He wrote her a letter.

PIP: Which she received when she was dressing for her marriage? At twenty minutes to nine?

HERBERT: At the hour and the minute.

PIP: She stopped all the clocks!

HERBERT: Yes – laid the whole house to waste as you have seen it and she has never since looked upon the light of day.

The young MISS HAVISHAM stays seated by her dressing table, stony faced, emotionless. Slowly the light fades on her.

It has been supposed that the man with whom she fell in love acted throughout in concert with her half brother; that it was a conspiracy between them and that they shared the profits.

And now Pip there is a perfectly open understanding between us. All that I know about Miss Havisham, you know.

PIP: And all that I know, you know.

SCENE 4

HERBERT is dressing himself and getting ready for work. We hear the sounds of the Calcutta streets from outside. His attention is averted when he hears an ostentatious cough. HERBERT looks up and sees JOE standing there. He is dressed uncharacteristically in his best dhoti and kurta which still looks a little threadbare and scruffy. HERBERT is taken aback by JOE's sudden appearance.

HERBERT: Ah – can I help you?

JOE: Joe Gargery – Mr Pip's friend – from the village.

HERBERT: How do you do – Joe Gargery. Well, well. I've heard so much about you. Do come in Joe!

JOE takes off his sandals but continues to stand in the doorway. He is staring at in amazement at the lodgings.

HERBERT: Please, come in!

JOE steps in tentatively. HERBERT enters. He looks surprised when he sees JOE.

HERBERT: Herbert Pocket, at your service sir.

HERBERT puts out his hand but JOE eyes the hand cautiously and instead does a namasté. HERBERT does namasté back.

JOE: Your servant Sahib. Is Mr Pip at home?

HERBERT: Yes. I believe he's just taking a bath. But he should be out any moment.

(Calls out.) Pip! Pip! You have a very important visitor!

Do you take tea or coffee Mr Gargery?

JOE: I'll take whichever is most agreeable to yourself.

HERBERT: What do you say to coffee?

JOE: I will not run contrary to your own opinions. But don't you never find it a little overheating?

HERBERT: Some tea then.

HERBERT pours some tea and hands it to JOE.

HERBERT: When did you come to town Mr Gargery?

JOE: Was it yesterday afternoon? Now it wasn't…yes, it was. Yes. It was yesterday afternoon.

HERBERT: Have you seen anything of Calcutta yet?

JOE: Yes.

HERBERT: And? What did you think?

JOE: It's full of buildings.

PIP enters wearing a smoking jacket.

PIP: Joe! This *is* a surprise. How are you?

JOE: Well. You have grown and swelled and…

JOE takes in the silk smoking jacket.

…look so different!

PIP: And you look wonderfully well.

JOE: To be sure you are an honour to your queen and country.

There is an awkward silence. JOE spills his tea. PIP fusses around and dabs at JOE's dhoti. It is obvious to JOE and HERBERT that PIP is deeply embarrassed by JOE's presence. JOE rather ostentatiously scratches his balls, sits cross legged on the chair and slurps his tea noisily. PIP is embarrassed.

HERBERT: Well, I must be off to work. Delighted to meet you Mr Gargery.

JOE: And you Sahib.

JOE does another namasté and HERBERT exits.

JOE: Now we are alone Sahib…

PIP: How can you call me Sahib!

JOE: …and since I can't stay many minutes more I just wanted to tell you something.

JOE falls silent and awkward.

PIP: What is it Joe? Tell me.

JOE: Biddy said it would be for the best if I came in person. Miss Havisham sent for me…but that is not why I came…

PIP: Miss Havisham?

JOE: I wanted to tell you in person. I am sorry to say…that is…I am, I am…Your poor dear sister has gone to the other life.

PIP: She's, she's…?

JOE: Yes Pip. Yama came in his chariot and took her away. She did not suffer, passed away in her sleep. The night before she had been in good cheer and she even said your name out loud.

PIP sits and hangs his head. JOE is quite choked.

JOE: Such a fine figure of a woman she was.

PIP: You came all the way to tell me?

JOE: I couldn't do it in a letter. Seemed heartless.

PIP: I am so sorry Joe.

JOE: Biddy has been a great comfort to me.

PIP: How is she?

JOE: She is fine. We talk of you often in the little kitchen and wonder what you are doing. We have done all the religious rites, Pumblechook saw to that.

PIP: I should have been there.

JOE: We had to cremate her. We couldn't wait.

PIP looks upset.

JOE: I also came here to be of some use to you. I was called to see Miss Havisham.

PIP: Were you?

JOE: Yes I was. I cleaned myself up and off I went.

She asked me if I was in correspondence with you. And I said yes I was although in a manner or speaking, it's Biddy that's in correspondence with you, I just speak…because I can't, as you know, write too well…

PIP: *(Irritated.)* I did try and teach you.

JOE: I know but I was always a bit dull.

PIP: You should have made more of an effort. You gave up too easily. But it's my fault too, I should have persevered.

JOE looks away hurt.

What did Miss Havisham say?

JOE: She said to tell you that Estella has come home and would be glad to see you in Calcutta.

PIP turns away in confusion and delight.

JOE: When I asked Biddy to write to you, she hung back a little and told me it's holiday time and you might want to see me and that you would be very glad to have it by word of mouth.

JOE hovers for a while as PIP takes in the news.

JOE: And Pip, I wish you good health, prosperity and Kali's blessings.

PIP: But you can't go now.

JOE: Yes. I must.

PIP: But you are coming back to dinner Joe?

JOE: No, I am not Pip.

JOE puts on his sandals and hugs PIP again briefly.

Pip *beta* life is made of ever so many partings all joined together. If there's been any fault today, it's mine. We're not two men who should be meeting in the city. We are old friends you and I and understand each other. It's not that I'm proud but I want to be right and you will never see me in these clothes again. I'm wrong in these clothes. I'm wrong away from my work bench. You wouldn't see half so much fault in me if you were to come and visit me in the village and see me in my *lunghi* with my work tools. Bless you Pip.

JOE touches PIP on the forehead in blessing and exits.

SCENE 5

PIP stands, dressed in his best suit, waiting impatiently. We hear the sound of a carriage arriving. ESTELLA enters. She looks up at PIP who does not recognise her at first. ESTELLA holds his surprised gaze.

PIP: Miss …Memsahib Estella!

ESTELLA puts her hand out which PIP takes and kisses. He is flustered.

ESTELLA: Please, it's Estella, we are equals.

PIP: Estella…It's a real pleasure seeing you. I have so looked forward to meeting you again for a long, long time…How was your journey?

ESTELLA: Tolerable. How are you Pip?

PIP: I am well – thank you. And Miss Havisham?

ESTELLA doesn't answer.

ESTELLA: Do you find me much changed, Pip?

PIP: At first, I thought there was nothing of Estella in the face or figure; but now it all settles so curiously into the old…

ESTELLA: What? You are not going to say into the old Estella? She was proud and insulting and you wanted to get away from her. Don't you remember?

PIP: That was a long time ago and I didn't know any better then.

ESTELLA: I don't doubt that you were right. I was horrible and very disagreeable.

PIP: Am I changed?

ESTELLA: Very much.

PIP: Less coarse and common?

ESTELLA laughs.

PIP: So, Estella, you have been in London?

ESTELLA: Yes. And Paris.

PIP: And how did you like it?

ESTELLA: It was wonderful. I enjoyed it very much… especially Paris…so many diverting entertainments. The opera…the ballet…the balls…

I seem to recall you having a fight in the garden with a pale faced boy.

PIP: Yes, Herbert Pocket!

ESTELLA: I must have been a singular little creature to hide and see that fight that day: but I did and I enjoyed it very much.

PIP: You rewarded me.

ESTELLA: Did I? I remember I entertained a great objection to your adversary because I wanted the Indian boy to triumph over the English boy.

PIP: Really?

ESTELLA: And I didn't like the idea that he should be brought here to pester me. He was so…unreasonably cheerful…

PIP: He still is! He and I are great friends now.

ESTELLA: Where are you staying?

PIP: In lodgings with Herbert.

ESTELLA: I am to have a carriage and you are to take me to South Calcutta. This is my purse and you are to pay my charges out of it.

ESTELLA hands over a purse to PIP.

PIP: No, I couldn't possibly.

ESTELLA: You must take the purse! We have no choice you and I but to obey our instructions. We are not free to follow our own devices you and I.

PIP: A carriage will have to be sent for. Will you wait here a while?

ESTELLA: I am to take some tea and rest and you are to take care of me whilst I wait.

PIP shows ESTELLA to a table and chairs. He calls over an Indian waiter.

PIP: Where are you going to in South Calcutta?

ESTELLA: I am going to live at great expense with a lady there who has the power – or says she has – of taking me about and introducing me and showing people to me and showing me to people.

PIP: Sounds like you will enjoy being admired.

ESTELLA does not answer.

ESTELLA: How do you thrive with Herbert?

PIP: I live quite pleasantly there; at least as pleasantly as I could anywhere away from you.

ESTELLA: You silly boy. How can you talk such nonsense?

PIP takes ESTELLA's hand and kisses it.

ESTELLA: You ridiculous boy.

PIP: Have you no heart?

ESTELLA: You must know that I have no heart.

PIP: I don't believe that.

ESTELLA: I have a heart to be stabbed or shot, I have no doubt and of course if it ceased to beat I should cease to be. But I have no softness there – no sympathy, sentiment, no nonsense.

PIP: But Estella...

ESTELLA: I am serious. If we are to be thrown much together, you had better believe it at once. I have not bestowed my tenderness anywhere. I have never had any such thing.

PIP: But at least...may I call on you from time to time...

ESTELLA: Yes. You are to see me. You are to come when
you think proper; you are to be mentioned to the family;
indeed you are already mentioned.

PIP: I'm surprised that Miss Havisham could bear to part with
you again so soon.

ESTELLA: It is part of Miss Havisham's plans for me Pip. I am
to write to her constantly and report how I get on – I and
the jewels – they are nearly all mine now.

PIP looks quizzically at ESTELLA.

ESTELLA: I wanted to ask you Pip. How do you enjoy being
an English man now?

PIP: Now you are mocking me.

ESTELLA: No, I am curious, that's all.

PIP: I feel at once included in the world of our rulers but at the
same time, I cannot enter the clubs or go to the races with
Herbert. Those are strictly reserved for the pure blooded
English. I am a strange man, Indian by birth but aping the
English.

ESTELLA: Pure blooded…

PIP: I exist in a kind of nether world.

ESTELLA: Poor Pip.

PIP: Now, you are definitely mocking me.

ESTELLA: You and I are not so different. Neither of us belong
in either world. We both have our lives planned and
shaped by others hands. We are not free.

PIP: Surely Estella…?

ESTELLA: Enough – please…I am here to enter Calcutta
society and you are to be my chaperone.

PIP: Is that all I am to you?

ESTELLA: I am only interested in one thing and that is to do as I am told. I am to make the acquaintance of a Mr Bentley Drummle whose sister I met in London and – I am here to party.

SCENE 6

It is late at night and PIP is sat on his own reading in his quarters by lamp light. He hears some noise on the stairs below, heavy trudging feet and a knock.

PIP: Herbert?

VOICE: *(OS.)* Mr Pip?

PIP: *(Calls out.)* That is my name.

PIP opens the door and an old man enters. He is dressed traditionally with a simple turban on his head but he has a Kashmiri shawl almost entirely obscuring his face.

PIP holds the lamp up.

PIP: How can I help you?

The OLD MAN looks at PIP full of affection. He holds out both his hands to PIP.

PIP: What is your business?

The OLD MAN looks momentarily disappointed.

OLD MAN: My Business? Ah yes! I will be explaining my business, by your leave.

PIP: Do you wish to come in?

OLD MAN: Yes.

PIP stands aside reluctantly as the OLD MAN enters. He wanders around the room looking and marvelling and muttering happily under his breath. PIP watches him uneasily.

OLD MAN: It is disappointing to a man after looking forward so much and coming so far…but you are not to blame for that – neither of us are to blame for that. I'll be speaking in a moment. Please … a moment.

The OLD MAN sits down without being asked. Once again, PIP is irritated.

OLD MAN: There's no one nearby is there?

PIP: Why do you a stranger come into my rooms at this time of night and ask that question?

The OLD MAN shakes his head and smiles.

OLD MAN: I'm glad you are growing up boy.

You acted noble, my boy. Noble Pip! And I have never forgotten it.

He turns and holds out his hands again. PIP recognises the OLD MAN as MAGWITCH. PIP stumbles back as MAGWITCH tries to hug PIP.

PIP: Keep away! If you are grateful to me for what I did when I was a little child, I hope you have shown your gratitude by mending your way of life. If you have come here to thank me, it was unnecessary. Surely you must understand that I…

PIP trails off.

MAGWITCH: You was saying that surely I must understand?

PIP: That I cannot wish to renew that chance meeting I had with you long ago. Our ways are different ways…

MAGWITCH looks hurt. PIP relents.

You look tired. Can I get you a drink?

MAGWITCH nods. PIP pours MAGWITCH a drink which he knocks back. MAGWITCH looks at PIP full of feeling.

PIP: I'm sorry if I spoke harshly to you just now. I wish you well and happy.

PIP pours MAGWITCH and himself another drink.

MAGWITCH nods and wipes his eyes with his sleeve.

PIP: How are you living?

MAGWITCH: Tea plantations in Assam.

PIP: I hope you've done well?

MAGWITCH: I've been doing wonderful well.

PIP: I am glad to hear it.

MAGWITCH: May I be so bold as to ask *you* how you have been doing so well since you and I were out alone in those remote crematorium grounds?

PIP: *(Very wary.)* I came into some property.

MAGWITCH: What property?

PIP: I don't know.

MAGWITCH: Whose property?

PIP: I don't know.

MAGWITCH: Do you have a guardian? A lawyer whose name, maybe, begins with erm…the letter 'J'?

PIP stands up and looks wildly at MAGWITCH.

MAGWITCH: Let's say that the employer of that lawyer whose name is beginning with 'J' and might be Jaggers – let's say he is coming down from the hills and wanted to come to you and wrote to Mr Jaggers clerk whose name might be….Wemick?

PIP is speechless.

MAGWITCH: Yes, my Pip, I've made an English gentleman of you! It's me that is doing it! I swore that time, that every rupee I earned would go to you. If I got rich, so would you. I escaped again and made for the hills. I worked hard, lived rough, changed my name. I speculated and now I own an entire tea plantation. I have a lot of money now and you kept me alive Pip.

PIP almost collapses in the chair. MAGWITCH goes down on bended knee and grasps PIP's hands in his. PIP tries not to recoil.

MAGWITCH: Pip. I've put away money for you to spend. Everytime I ate, and every night before I fell asleep, I would see your face looking at me. That poor orphan, low caste boy…the cobbler's boy…And now I am looking at you! Looking at these lodgings of yours. Fit for a King.

MAGWITCH wanders around the room and picks up books.

And you can read all these English books can you? You shall read them to me Pip! I'll be proud that I made you into a gentleman.

PIP is silent.

MAGWITCH: But did you never think it might be me?

PIP: Never. Never.

MAGWITCH: It was me and single handed. Never a soul knew except me and Mr Jaggers.

PIP: Was there no one else?

MAGWITCH: No. Who else should there be? And Pip, how good looking you've grown.

MAGWITCH looks at PIP full of love.

MAGWITCH: All I want to do is to stand here and look at you. Look, all I have is yours.

MAGWITCH desperately pulls out a pocket book and shows PIP papers.

There's more…much more…property…and land as well as the plantation and the profits…Curse on you every one – you white faced devils…you corrupt judges and trampler of decent folk! I'll show you a better gentleman than the whole kit of you put together. I'll make you into a *Chief* Pip…no! A *Maharajah.*

I had to come back to see you once more. It wasn't easy or safe for me to leave the plantation. No one must know I'm here. No-one. But I did it Pip. I did it!

I must be cautious but it's worth taking the risk…to be seeing my boy…my boy….

PIP: Stop! Why isn't it safe?

MAGWITCH: I was sent to the Andaman islands for life.

It's death for me to be coming back here. I will be hanged if they catch me.

PIP: Hanged?

HERBERT POCKET enters. When MAGWITCH sees HERBERT he pulls a knife from his belt but PIP notices him.

PIP: No! This is my friend!

MAGWITCH hesitates before putting away his knife.

PIP: Herbert. This is Herbert Pocket.

HERBERT does a namasté. MAGWITCH looks suspicious.

PIP: He is the closest thing I have in this world to a brother.

MAGWITCH: *(Incredulous.)* A *sahib*?

PIP: Yes. We share lodgings here…

It's because of you…your money brought us together.

PIP: Herbert, this is my benefactor.

MAGWITCH laughs heartily and then approaches HERBERT, hugging him and slapping him on the back. HERBERT is stunned.

MAGWITCH: Look at you Pip – you *are* an English gentleman. Sharing lodgings with a Sahib!

MAGWITCH sits down. HERBERT tries to pull himself together.

PIP: I don't even know your name. I don't know anything about you – where you're from, why you were a convict…

MAGWITCH: You want to know about me?

PIP: Yes. Of course.

MAGWITCH: I suppose you have a right to know.

(To HERBERT.) Swear, as Pip's brother, you will keep quiet about what I reveal to you?

PIP: We both swear.

MAGWITCH: I want to hear *him* say it!

HERBERT: You have my word.

MAGWITCH: And remember one thing – whatever I did in the past – I've paid for it. I've been punished. I've done my time.

PIP and HERBERT listen.

MAGWITCH: My *Pip* and Pip's brother… in jail, out of jail, in jail, out of jail. There – that's *my* life. I've been locked up, beaten, whipped, carted here, shipped there…I don't even know where I was born. I first became aware of myself down by the sea in Cape Colony, stealing fish from the fishermen. I know my name was Magwitch and my first name – Abel. I grew up somehow, thieving, scrounging, begging. I was caught by the soldiers and thrown in jail and was known as a 'hard one'. "This one's a hardened one". They'd say to prison visitors "Lives in jails". And the visitors would give me Bibles to read and would talk about things I couldn't understand. They always went on about the Devil.

PIP and HERBERT share an awkward look.

Tramping, begging, thieving, working sometimes, poaching, labouring, driving wagons, this is how I grew to be a man. At one point they banished me to Robben Island where they send convicts and lepers. When I was released I got a job as a sailor, travelled the world, treated harshly on those Colonist ships. Beaten again, starved, abused.

I jumped ship in Calcutta and liked it here. I met a woman and…

MAGWITCH stops full of emotion and looks around the room wildly for a moment.

MAGWITCH: At the races, I was working as a horse handler. I was good with horses and got paid for the work. There I got acquainted with a Sahib. His name – Compeyson.

HERBERT seems to recognise the name.

MAGWITCH: He was the other convict you saw me fighting Pip.

Soon, I was running jobs for him. He was a good looking, smooth talking gentleman. Nice manners, way with words – you know the type. But he was a swindler, handwriting forger, dealing in stolen banknotes. His mind worked on trapping people and getting whatever he could out of them for his own means. He had no heart.

He had this man working for him – a half breed – Arthur Havisham – English name but he was brown skinned. Him and Compeyson had been in a bad thing with a rich lady some years back. This lady was Arthur's half sister. They made a lot of money out of her and then lost it all.

MAGWITCH: Soon after Arthur died, I became Compeyson's slave.

I was always in trouble, getting in debt to him and doing his dirty work. He had craft and he had learning and he had no mercy. My wife and I were having a hard enough time with the…

MAGWITCH stops himself again and looks around wildly again.

MAGWITCH: Eventually we were caught and I was tried with Compeyson for felony – putting stolen bank notes into circulation.

They made out I was the guilty one who had led Compeyson by the nose. Compeyson was English, he had character and learning whilst what was I? Black, history of crime and no character. He got seven and I got fourteen years.

We were in the same prison ship but I couldn't get at him. Then I escaped and was hiding in that crematorium when I saw my boy.

MAGWITCH looks at PIP with great affection.

When my boy told me that Compeyson was out too, that's when I grabbed him. I would have been happy to let the river Goddess embrace us for eternity if those soldiers hadn't turned up.

HERBERT: Where is he now?

MAGWITCH: I never heard of him again.

Pip my boy, I am tired. I've had a long journey… tomorrow we will talk.

PIP: It isn't safe for you to go away tonight. You can't risk it. You must stay the night here.

MAGWITCH: You have a bed for me?

PIP: You can have mine. I will sleep in here tonight.

MAGWITCH: Thank you. It's so good to see you again Pip.

My son. My true son.

PIP is unable to respond.

Lead the way Pip. Lead the way.

PIP leads MAGWITCH and they both exit.

HERBERT paces for a few moments, trying to take it all in. PIP re-enters.

HERBERT: My poor, dear Pip. I am too stunned to think.

PIP: I can't believe it…it's too awful to imagine.

HERBERT looks at PIP with empathy.

He's a criminal…a convicted man…and everything I have become…my great expectations…

PIP sits and tears at his hair.

HERBERT: Pip my friend, you mustn't take it so badly.

PIP: I assumed my benefactor was Miss Havisham!

HERBERT: We all thought that.

PIP: And Estella was never meant for me. She was never part of my inheritance. What a fool I've been.

HERBERT: That name, Compeyson. I knew I had heard it before. He was Miss Havisham's suitor! The man who jilted her at the altar.

PIP: And Arthur was her half brother.

Then if I never take another penny from him think what I owe him already? I am heavily in debt – very heavily for me who has no expectations and I have been bred to no calling and I am fit for nothing.

HERBERT: Don't say that.

PIP breaks down and cries. HERBERT hugs him and tries to comfort PIP.

HERBERT: Let's think this through…there must be a solution to the problem…if he is recognised and caught…

PIP: I would be responsible for his death.

I only knew him as the miserable wretch who terrified me for two days in my childhood.

HERBERT: You must get him out of Calcutta before you stir a finger to extricate yourself. Once he's gone, out of harms way, get yourself away from his money and we'll see it out together.

PIP: I will save him. But first, I must see Estella. I will travel tonight, immediately to Miss Havisham's.

HERBERT: You can't leave now. It is too dangerous!

PIP: Please Herbert. Give me one day. When I return I will arrange Magwitch's affairs.

HERBERT: Pip, this is madness!

PIP: Herbert, it is imperative that I speak to Estella and Miss Havisham.

PIP exits.

HERBERT looks distraught.

SCENE 7

ESTELLA and MISS HAVISHAM are sat back in MISS HAVISHAM's room ESTELLA is working on some embroidery. PIP enters. He stands before the two women. MISS HAVISHAM looks older, more shrunken now.

PIP: What I have to say to Estella, Miss Havisham, I will say before you, presently…It will not displease you, it may not surprise you…I am as unhappy as you can ever have meant me to be.

ESTELLA does not look up.

PIP: But please do one thing for me Miss Havisham.

Prove to me you are not entirely heartless.

MISS HAVISHAM: I don't have to prove anything to you.

PIP: Herbert and Matthew Pocket are not self seeking. They are good people.

MISS HAVISHAM: They are *your* friends.

PIP: You deeply wrong them if you suppose them to be otherwise than generous, upright, open and incapable of anything designing or mean. They are not like you.

MISS HAVISHAM: What do you want?

PIP: If you could, spare the money to do my friend

Herbert a lasting service in life. Help him set up a partnership but do it without letting him know I asked for it.

MISS HAVISHAM: What else?

PIP: When you first brought me here Miss Havisham I suppose I really only came as a kind of a servant, to gratify a want or a whim and to be paid for it?

MISS HAVISHAM: You did.

PIP: And Mr Jaggers…

MISS HAVISHAM: Mr Jaggers had nothing to do with it. His being my lawyer and the lawyer of your patron is a coincidence.

PIP: But when I mistakenly supposed you to be my patron, you led me on?

MISS HAVISHAM: Yes.

PIP: Was that kind?

MISS HAVISHAM: Who am I for God's sake that I should be kind?

You have made your own snares. *I* never made them.

PIP: Estella. You know I love you. You know that I have always loved you.

ESTELLA looks at PIP emotionless.

MISS HAVISHAM: How can you expect her to love *you*? Estella needs to marry someone worthy of her station in life.

PIP: It was cruel in Miss Havisham, horribly cruel, to practise on the susceptibility of a poor boy and to torture me through all these years I think in the endurance of her own trial, she forgot mine Estella.

MISS HAVISHAM looks horrified and puts her hand to her heart.

ESTELLA: When you say you love me, I know what you mean, as a form of words: but nothing more. I don't care for what you say at all. I warned you.

PIP: I thought and hoped you could not mean it. You, so young, untried and beautiful Estella. Surely it is not Nature.

ESTELLA: It is in *my* nature. It is in the nature formed within me.

PIP: Is it true that Bentley Drummle is in town here and pursuing you?

ESTELLA: It is true.

PIP: You cannot love him Estella!

ESTELLA: What have I told you? I cannot love.

But we are to be married.

MISS HAVISHAM looks pained.

PIP covers his face in his hands and looks utterly distraught. He collects himself.

PIP: Estella, dearest Estella, do not let Miss Havisham lead you into this fatal step. Put me aside forever – you have done so I know but bestow yourself on some worthier person than Drummle.

ESTELLA: I have agreed to marry him. The preparations for my wedding have begun.

PIP: He's a brute!

ESTELLA: My adopted mother does not want me to get married so soon. But I am tired of this life and want a change.

MISS HAVISHAM: So hard! So hard!

ESTELLA: Who taught me to be hard? Who praised me when I learnt my lesson?

MISS HAVISHAM: But to be hard on people who love you?

ESTELLA: You taught me. You showed me from the dawn of my intelligence that daylight was made to be my enemy and destroyer and that I must avoid it, for it had blighted you and would else blight me. I must be taken as I have been made by you. A proud, English lady. Someone who rules without mercy. Surely, you should be delighted at how I've turned out?

PIP: Estella. Please listen to me.

ESTELLA: Pip, we will never understand each other. Let us part as friends. You will get over me in time.

PIP: Never Estella.

ESTELLA: Nonsense. I will be out of your thoughts soon enough.

PIP: Out of my thoughts? You are part of my existence, part of myself. You have been in every line I have ever read, since I first came here, the rough common Indian boy whose poor heart you wounded even then. You have been in every prospect I have ever seen since – on the river, on the sails of the ships, in the clouds, in the light, in the darkness, in the winds, in the wood, in the sea, in the streets. Estella, to the last hour of my life, you cannot choose but remain part of my character, part of the little good in me, part of the evil. But in this separation, I associate you only with the good. Kali bless you and forgive you.

PIP turns and leaves. ESTELLA looks amazed as he walks away whilst MISS HAVISHAM looks full of remorse.

SCENE 8

It is late and PIP is hurrying home through the dark streets of Calcutta. He is stopped by WEMICK.

WEMICK: Don't go home Mr Pip.

PIP is startled. He peers into the dark as WEMICK comes forward.

PIP: Wemick!

WEMICK: Now Mr Pip, you and I understand each other. I accidentally heard yesterday morning that a certain person of tea plantation pursuits had made a little stir in certain parts of the city where he shouldn't be. I have also heard that your lodgings are being watched.

PIP: Who told you this?

WEMICK: I wouldn't go into that. It might clash with official responsibilities. You have heard of a man of bad character, whose real name is Compeyson?

PIP: He lives?

WEMICK: Right here in this city. So, I went to your lodgings and told your friend Herbert that if he was aware of any Ram, Krishna or Hari being about your lodgings, he had better get Ram, Krishna or Hari out of the way.

PIP: Herbert must have been…

WEMICK: Beside himself but then he said he could find a secret place to hide away.

Whispers an address in PIP's ear.

WEMICK: Make sure that you avail yourself of portable property and cash. You don't know what may happen to Ram or Krishna…get him out of the city…if he is arrested, all his goods revert to the Crown. There will be no more property.

PIP: Thank you…thank you…

WEMICK does namasté, gives PIP a note and disappears into the dark.

SCENE 9

MAGWITCH and HERBERT are sat in a room together playing cards. PIP is standing by the window peering anxiously out. MAGWITCH hums a tune as he plays. (It is the same song PIP heard ESTELLA humming many years ago). PIP recognises the tune from somewhere but can't place it. He finds it hard to settle and keeps going to the window and pacing.

MAGWITCH: Sit down. You are making me nervous.

PIP: I just want to make sure...

MAGWITCH: If that scoundrel is watching this house, you would not be able to see him. He is very good at hiding.

PIP: Why do you think Compeyson is still after you?

MAGWITCH: He's heard I have money. That's all he cares about – all he ever cared about.

HERBERT: There are many people like him in the world.

MAGWITCH: Money is power though. Why else you white men come all the way here? Stealing land here, there everywhere, making us slave for you in our own countries.

HERBERT: You hate us don't you?

MAGWITCH: Not all of you. You are Pip's brother and you are a surprise to me. My experience of the white man you understand has never been very favourable. They are always telling us we are not as clever, not as civilised, we are dirty, stupid and in the end, we believe them. We think that we are inferior just because they tell us we are – that we can never hold our head high.

PIP listens with interest.

One day the white man will be run out of this place. And it'll be a shock to them. My boy Pip, with his education will teach them a lesson.

PIP: Is that why you helped me? For revenge?

MAGWITCH: No. No my boy. You reminded me of someone. When I saw you out there in that crematorium, you were such a little thing. You told me you were an orphan.

HERBERT: Reminded you of who?

MAGWITCH: I had a baby girl. Her mother was Indian. She and I...but she was a jealous type...she had violence in her...thought I was seeing some other woman when I wasn't. She had a row with this woman...killed her.

HERBERT: Murder?

MAGWITCH: Jaggers pleaded her case and got her off but this woman of mine...so jealous and angry with me...she took my baby girl away from me... said she gave her away... I never saw her again.

HERBERT: And Pip reminded you...?

MAGWITCH: I loved that little girl like I never loved anything before. Three years old last time I saw her. Don't know what happened to her. Never found my wife again.

MAGWITCH looks furious.

MAGWITCH: That's how he had a hold on me.

HERBERT: Who?

MAGWITCH: Compeyson. Said he knew where my little girl was. Said he'd bring her to me if I did one last job for him...kept promising...kept making me do one last job for him...

Compeyson. Sent down by the Gods to do evil on this earth. If I ever find him, his day of reckoning will come. I will destroy Compeyson once and for all.

PIP: Magwitch, we have to get you away from here. I don't want this Compeyson to catch up with you.

SCENE 10

MISS HAVISHAM is sat by a lamp. PIP rushes in.

PIP: Mr Jaggers gave me your note yesterday.

MISS HAVISHAM: Ahhh – Pip – you came.

PIP: He said it was urgent…but I really can't stay long.

MISS HAVISHAM: I want to pursue that subject you mentioned to me when you were last here, and to show you that I am not all stone. What does Mr Pocket Junior wish to do?

PIP: He wants to set up a partnership for the insurance of ships.

MISS HAVISHAM: But he doesn't own any ships!

PIP: Precisely.

MISS HAVISHAM: How much money is needed for this venture?

PIP: Nine hundred pounds.

MISS HAVISHAM: I keep no money here but I will send you the sum.

PIP: Thank you Miss Havisham.

MISS HAVISHAM writes something on a piece of paper and hands the paper over to PIP.

MISS HAVISHAM: Can I only serve you Pip by serving your friend?

Is there nothing I can do for you?

PIP: There is nothing.

MISS HAVISHAM: Will you ever forgive me in the future Pip?

PIP: I can forgive you now.

MISS HAVISHAM drops to her feet and touches PIP's feet in pranam.

MISS HAVISHAM: You have shown me mercy.

PIP tries to lift MISS HAVISHAM up but instead, she grabs his hands and kisses them and cries.

MISS HAVISHAM: What have I done? What have I done? Until you spoke to her the other day and until I saw in you a looking glass that showed me what I once felt myself, I did not know what I had done. What have I done? What have I done? What have I done?

PIP finally manages to help MISS HAVISHAM up and back into her chair.

PIP: Miss Havisham, if you can ever undo any scrap of what you have done to Estella in keeping her right nature away from her, you should do it.

MISS HAVISHAM: It is too late. She is married to Drummle now.

When she first came here to me, I meant to save her from misery like my own. But then she grew…so beautiful…so innocent…I was afraid for her so I stole her heart away and put ice in its place.

PIP: Better to have left her a natural heart even to be bruised or broken. Whose child was Estella?

MISS HAVISHAM: Jaggers brought her here…he said she was the product of – an African man and an Indian maid. I never knew their names.

PIP: How old was Estella when she was brought here?

MISS HAVISHAM: Three years old.

PIP: You brought her up as an English woman. Does she know of her true heritage?

MISS HAVISHAM: She remembers her father. She was very close to him it seems.

PIP: She loved him.

MISS HAVISHAM: Yes. I wanted to fashion her into a woman that all men would desire but never gain.

PIP: It is you who are heartless then Miss Havisham.

You did a grevious thing in taking an impressionable child to cage up in a lightless world, to mould into the form of your wild resentment, spurned affection and wounded pride. In shutting out the light of day, you have shut out infinitely more. In seclusion you have secluded yourself from a thousand natural healing influences. Your mind grew diseased.

MISS HAVISHAM: Oh Pip. What have I done?

PIP turns and exits. MISS HAVISHAM stands up.

MISS HAVISHAM: *(Calls out.)* Pip! Pip! Please…what have I done!

What have I done!

As MISS HAVISHAM calls out, she knocks over the lamp. Her gown catches fire goes up in flames. She screams. PIP runs back and tries to beat the flames out with his bare hands, as the flames die, PIP holds MISS HAVISHAM.

MISS HAVISHAM: When she first came to me, I meant to save her from misery like mine.

Forgive me Pip.

What have I done?

MISS HAVISHAM faints in PIP's arms.

SCENE 11

PIP's hands are bandaged. He chases after JAGGERS as JAGGERS walks into his office, bundles of papers under his arm. WEMICK tries to keep pace.

PIP: How is Miss Havisham?

JAGGERS: She is very weak and the burns are not so bad – thanks to you. But she has taken to her bed.

PIP: I hope she recovers.

I did ask something of Miss Havisham, sir. I asked her to give me some information relative to her adoptive daughter and she gave me all she possessed.

JAGGERS: Did she?

PIP: And I have talked to my friend Ram in the tea plantation area of commerce who also told me something of her parentage.

He is her father.

JAGGERS stops and looks taken aback. WEMICK quickly closes the office door behind him.

JAGGERS: And does this Ram make this claim?

PIP: He does not. He has no knowledge or belief that his daughter exists.

JAGGERS: I admit nothing!

PIP: Tell me.

JAGGERS: I'll put a case to you. A wretched woman with a small child came for representation from a lawyer. Put the case this woman admitted murder. Put that this lawyer also held a trust to find a child for an eccentric rich lady to adopt and bring up.

PIP: I follow you.

JAGGERS: Put the case that this lawyer lived in an atmosphere of evil and that all he saw of children was their being generated in great numbers for certain destruction. Put the case that pretty well near all the children he saw in his daily business life, he had reason to look upon as so much spawn to develop into fish that were to come to his net – to be prosecuted, defended, forsworn, made orphans, be-devilled somehow.

WEMICK: Put the case that here was one pretty child out of the heap who could be saved; whom the father believed dead. Maybe the lawyer said to the woman, "I will take this child and give her a home with a proper English lady. I will represent you and if you are saved, your child is saved and if you are lost, your child is still saved".

PIP: I understand.

WEMICK: But we make no admissions.

JAGGERS: Admit to nothing.

WEMICK: Put the case that the child grew up and was married for money. That the mother was still living. That the father was still living but that neither mother nor father had any contact anymore.

JAGGERS: That the secret was still a secret, until you got wind of it. For whose sake would you reveal the secret? The father's? The mother's? The child's?

MOLLY enters. She picks up a tray of tea things, her arms bared. PIP stares at her suddenly realising she is ESTELLA's mother. MOLLY exits.

WEMICK: Who would benefit from knowing the truth?

PIP hangs his head.

JAGGERS: For whose sake?

JAGGERS pats PIP on the shoulder and exits.

WEMICK looks at PIP with feeling and follows JAGGERS.

SCENE 12

It is religious festival time 'Kali Puja'. People are dancing in the streets in honour of the Goddess Kali. Conch shells blare, drums, dancing etc. A statue of Kali is paraded through the streets as people celebrate. MAWITCH in disguise is bustled through the crowd by HERBERT and PIP.

PIP: If all goes well you will be free and safe again in a few hours.

MAGWITCH: I hope so. Although I cannot bare to be parted from you again.

PIP: But I am coming with you! We take the boat from here to…

MAGWITCH: With me?

PIP: Yes! I have very little here to stay for and you and I have a lot of catching up to do.

MAGWITCH: You would do this for me Pip?

PIP: When I saw you in that crematorium all those years ago, I was terrified of you. What I did, I did out of fear not kindness.

HERBERT: Come on Pip, we need to get to that boat. The crowd's picking up.

The crowd carries the effigy of Kali down towards the river and PIP and the others become entangled in the festivities.

A whistle blows and COMPEYSON points in the direction of MAGWITCH. He is followed by SOLDIERS. MAGWITCH turns and sees COMPEYSON. He roars with fury, grabs COMPEYSON and they start to fight. The crowd screams and disperses. As the struggle continues, MAGWITCH holds onto COMPEYSON and strangles him. The SOLDIERS shout at him but MAGWITCH holds COMPEYSON until COMPEYSON stops struggling.

As MAGWITCH gets up, the soldiers raise their guns at him.

SCENE 13

MAGWITCH lies on a bed in a prison cell. PIP enters and sits by MAGWITCH's side.

MAGWITCH: Jaggers tells me they mean to hang me next week. I know he tried his best.

PIP nods.

MAGWITCH: You've never deserted me.

Where is your Sahib brother?

PIP: He has gone to Bombay. He has bought two ships there and is setting up his business in the city.

MAGWITCH: He has already left?

PIP: He came to see you but you were feverish.

MAGWITCH: I am sorry for that. I liked him…not bad for a white man.

MAGWITCH laughs but the laughter end with a wracking cough.

PIP: You don't look well.

MAGWITCH: That last fight… I'm an old man now and not as strong as I was. But I am happy that Compeyson is gone from this world. He can't harm anyone else now.

PIP: Are you in much pain today?

MAGWITCH: I can't complain my Pip.

PIP: You never do.

MAGWITCH sinks deeper into his bed.

MAGWITCH: What makes me happy, is that you and I have become friends. You were such a little boy! And since I've been under a dark cloud, you and I have been even more comfortable together…

PIP: I wish we had more time.

MAGWITCH flinches with pain.

MAGWITCH: Use my money. I want you to be a proud and upright Indian. I want you to always hold your head high and never let them kick you like a dog, like they kicked me. All my life they looked down on me, always cursing and abusing. The English made me the monster I became. But you, you will be different!

PIP: I will.

MAGWITCH: You are a good young man – Pip. You have something like a light that is glowing inside you. I saw it in the crematorium.

PIP starts to cry.

MAGWITCH: Listen. You taught me to love again when all I saw was red rage and hatred around me. So, you must always remember that you are special. And I will watch over you from up there. No harm will come to my Pip because I will have a good talk with Lady Kali to make sure you are showered with good fortune.

PIP: Don't talk of leaving me.

MAGWITCH: I am so happy that we met again. And I wish that in the future you find nice bright eyes to love and nurture you. And also…

MAGWITCH tries to speak but his voice is growing fainter and PIP cannot hear him.

PIP: Don't speak. I want you to listen to what I have to say. You had a child once, whom you loved and lost.

MAGWITCH looks full of hope.

PIP: She lived and found powerful friends. She is living now. She is a lady and very beautiful. And I love her!

MAGWITCH reaches up and touches PIP's forehead and then he slumps.

PIP weeps.

SCENE 14

We are back in the village. JOE GARGERY is outside working on his shoes in the workshop. BIDDY is sorting through the rice. She is singing as JOE smiles and listens. We can hear the sounds of the countryside and the call of birds over head.

JOE: Shall I look in on him?

BIDDY: He is still sleeping, but the fever has lifted.

JOE: Thank Kali Ma. He was raving in his sleep.

Sounded wild and desolate last night. Wanted to hold him tight and tell him…

BIDDY: Tell him what?

JOE: That he has to live. After everything he's been through, he must pull through.

BIDDY: Stop worrying Joe. We will make him better.

JOE: When he's asleep – he looks like my little Pip again. Lips like this. Fists all clenched.

JOE impersonates PIP as a child. BIDDY laughs.

BIDDY: Been through a lot. He has to take it easy… has to stay here until he is completely recovered.

JOE: Has to wake up first.

BIDDY: He *will* wake up. Pip's a young man, strong…

I'm going to fetch some water from the well. Call me if he wakes.

BIDDY takes a large clay pot and walks down to the river.

PIP shuffles out of the hut and sees JOE. PIP is uneasy on his legs and JOE rushes forward to support him.

PIP: Is that you Joe?

JOE: It is. But you shouldn't be up. I've been so worried about you Pip, my boy. So good to see you here, back home. We're going to look after you. You're going to be better now.

PIP: Don't break my heart. Look angry at me. Strike me Joe. Tell me of my ingratitude. Don't be so good to me!

JOE sits PIP down in a chair, kneels and puts his arms around PIP.

JOE: Me and Biddy brought you home. We had word that you were ill, with a fever and debtors at your door.

PIP: I owe so much money…they came to arrest me.

JOE: Don't you worry about that.

PIP: Perhaps not now but…Is Miss Havisham dead Joe?

JOE: She isn't living anymore.

PIP: She begged my forgiveness.

JOE: I heard. Herbert told me in a letter which I read myself. She left him a handsome amount. Most of it went to Estella but she even left some money for you.

PIP: You can read?

JOE: Biddy taught me.

PIP: Where is Biddy?

JOE: She'll be back soon. She has been by your side night and day.

PIP: Dearest Biddy.

JOE: A good woman. The best.

PIP: You heard about who my true benefactor was?

JOE: Yes, but enough talking…

PIP: He was a man…a good man…and he is dead now…

PIP breaks down. JOE hugs PIP and rocks him as he cries.

PIP: I don't deserve your love. I don't deserve your affection. I have been so ungrateful and so quick to cast you off. All my opportunities wasted and gone. I've lost everything.

JOE: Shhhh…

PIP: I am so sorry. Forgive me.

JOE: Nothing to forgive. You will always be my *beta* and you will recover and you will make your life all over again. Only this time, you will be wiser.

PIP: What will I do? Where will I go? I am fit for nothing.

JOE: You must stay here for as long as you can bear it. Herbert sent word that as soon as you are recovered, you are to travel to Bombay, to work with him there. He said if you don't, he will come and fetch you himself.

BIDDY returns carrying water.

BIDDY screeches with joy when she sees PIP sitting there.

BIDDY: He is awake! Why didn't you tell me?!

BIDDY puts down her pot and rushes to PIP and hugs him.

PIP: Thanks to you Biddy. I hear you nursed me.

BIDDY: Joe never left your side.

PIP: You both look so fresh and young and…Oh Biddy. You look so beautiful. I was such a fool not to see that before… if only you will forgive me, maybe…

BIDDY stops PIP.

BIDDY: Pip. Joe has something important to tell you.

JOE looks nervous.

PIP: Yes Pip…Me and Biddy…well…we decided…well…that is…Biddy agreed…

BIDDY: We are married!

PIP looks from JOE to BIDDY in amazement. JOE nods happily.

PIP: Then dear Biddy, you have the best husband in the world. Biddy, forgive me for being unjust to you in the past. And Joe you have the best wife in the world and she will make you as happy as even you deserve to be, dear, good noble Joe.

They all hug and laugh together.

SCENE 15

We are back in the streets of Calcutta. We see the hustle and bustle of the street vendors and hawkers. A group stand by and watch a dancer whilst another man stands on a soap box and speaks to the crowd.

MAN: If we are so lowly, if our customs are so unworthy and backward, if our religions are ancient and our intellect so tiny, why do they bother with us? Why do they need to be here?

We must rise up brothers. We must break the shackles. Just as our brothers in 1857 tried to rebel against the foreign invaders, we must follow their example. But not through violence or hatred. We must do it through debate, through reason, through intellectual rigour. We must argue our case for our right to determine the affairs of our own country.

PIP enters. He is older now. He is walking and reminiscing with an older HERBERT. PIP is dressed in the traditional garments of an Indian man whilst HERBERT is dressed in a suit. PIP walks tall and looks comfortable in himself.

PIP: So many new buildings.

HERBERT: Remember that batty young woman who used to sell mangoes on the corner?

PIP: You loved her.

HERBERT: I loved her mangoes. I almost thought of proposing to her after a particularly tasty batch.

They both laugh heartily.

HERBERT: We spent too much money here.

PIP: I thought I'd never pay off.

HERBERT: Joe managed it all beautifully didn't he?

PIP: Never even told me. Kept me out of debtors prison.

HERBERT: You paid it off though. Every last penny. You heard Drummle died didn't you?

PIP: I read about it in the papers. Trampled by a horse over some fight with the owner.

HERBERT: Very shady.

PIP: Where did you say we are meeting Clara and the boys?

HERBERT: At the coffee shop.

PIP: Our old haunt?

HERBERT: It's all been done up now. Marble floors no less!

ESTELLA walks by. Both she and PIP stop in their tracks when they see each other.

ESTELLA: Is that really you Pip?

PIP: Estella!

HERBERT bows and makes a hasty retreat.

ESTELLA is changed. She is wearing an African wrap now, is softer and more worn with time.

ESTELLA: I am greatly changed. I wonder you know me.

And you, you still live in Bombay?

PIP: Still. Herbert and I were back for a visit.

ESTELLA: You do well?

PIP: I work hard and yes – I do pretty well.

ESTELLA: I have often thought of you.

PIP: Have you?

ESTELLA: Of late, very often. There was a long hard time when I kept far from me the remembrance of you. I am married again. To an Indian doctor. Are you…?

PIP: No.

ESTELLA: Suffering has been stronger than all other teaching and has taught me to understand what your heart used to be. I have been bent and broken but I hope – into better shape.

I never forgot what you said to me that night and how I threw it away. I was ignorant of its worth.

PIP nods and they gaze at each other for some time.

ESTELLA: I am sorry for…

I regretted it for many, many years.

Be as considerate and good to me as you were, and tell me we are friends.

PIP: We are friends.

You will always have a place in my heart.

ESTELLA: And you in mine.

They shake hands tenderly, holding hands for a little too long. Eventually they part, walking slowly away from each other.

THE END.